Architecturally Speaking

By Eugene Raskin

Illustrations by Robert Osborn

Reinhold Publishing Corporation

Contents

If he contend, as sometimes he will contend, that he has defined all his terms and proved all his propositions, then either he is a performer of logical miracles or he is an ass; and as you know, logical miracles are impossible.

—Cassius J. Keyser, *Mathematical Philosophy*

To Raya

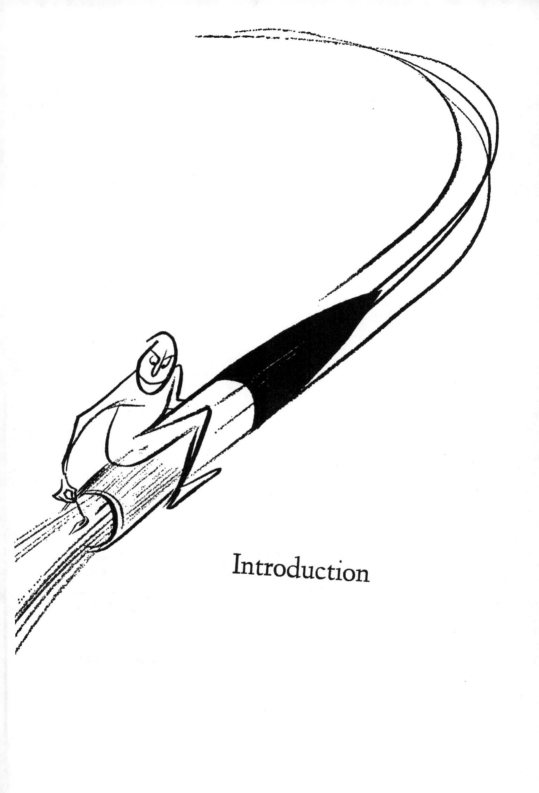

Introduction

It seems obvious, once stated, that in a human class of life, the linguistic, structural and semantic issues represent powerful and ever present environmental factors, which constitute most important components of all our problems.

—Alfred H. Korzybski, *Science and Sanity*

Introduction

OUR PRESENT UNDERSTANDING OF OUR universe and ourselves, while still pathetically small, has been vastly enlarged by the work of Minkowski, Einstein, and the inventors of the quantum theories, whose postulates have generally replaced the traditional Newtonian-Euclidian-Aristotelian ones. Many long-standing problems, including that of the atom, have become suddenly capable of solution now that a new method of approaching them has been stated.

Such a statement required linguistic revision, of course, since the older language contained no terms suitable for the new formulations.* The language of mathematics, for example, underwent (on the higher level) many drastic changes in the process of including and using the new expressions that were invented to symbolize the new structural and relational theories being presented. Physics, chemistry, genetics, astronomy,

* "The structure of the world happens to be such that empirically 'matter,' 'space,' 'time,' cannot be divided; wherefore, we should have a . . . language of similar structure. This was accomplished by Einstein-Minkowski, when they created a language of 'space-time,' in which the hard lumps against which we bump our noses are connected analytically with the curvature of 'space-time.'" Alfred H. Korzybski, *Science and Sanity*, The International Non-Aristotelian Library Publishing Company.

biochemistry, bacteriology, in fact, all fields of scientific inquiry in which mathematics is used, were profoundly revolutionized. What had been considered known became unknown, what were facts became fictions, and much that had been mysterious was a mystery no longer; the impossible not only became possible but turned into operating realities overnight.

A striking characteristic common to all the revolutions in the various sciences was the inclusion, for the first time, of the "observer" as an inescapable part of all calculations, formulations, structural and relational postulates. Since the act of measuring, for instance, requires a measurer, using a measuring unit of his own invention and *choosing* what to measure and when to stop measuring, it is meaningless to speak of anything as having dimension, objectively. A stated dimension makes sense only if the methods, choices, and purposes of the measurer (observer) are included as an integral part of the quantity.

A calculation, too, requires a calculator, who, necessarily, is equipped with doctrines, intentions, and methods. Without the doctrines (mathematical assumptions), intentions, and methods, his calculations are meaningless.

In short, science, with all its theories, experiments, calculations, and conclusions, has been accepted as a *phenomenon of human behavior* along with painting, poetry, digestion, and the production of babies.

This seemingly simple step has had tremendous consequences and will have many more. Aside from the fields of study already mentioned, medicine (in its researches into psychosomatic factors) and psychiatry have made great strides by abandoning their former elementalistic approach to symptoms in favor of considering the human being from the organism-as-a-whole standpoint. Illness, too, is a phenomenon of human behavior, not to be looked upon as a matter of *pure* chemistry, bacteriology, or neurology.

Although the stars and the microbes are not man made (it is only our understanding of them that is our doing), there can be no question about architecture; it is a result of human behavior all the way through. Architecture is man-built, man-used, and man-appreciated. It is also sometimes man-wrecked, man-misused, and man-disliked. To treat of architecture without considering the psychological and physiological characteristics of those by whom and for whom it is created makes no more sense than a discussion of the Bach fugues between two baboons, neither of whom has ever heard one.

Yet just as scientists for many centuries spoke of physical quantities as though they had an absolute objective reality without reference to the doctrines, methods, and capacities of the humans measuring them, so architects and critics have spoken of architecture as though it were a thing apart from man. They have looked upon "scale," "rhythm," "proportion," etc., as though they existed all by themselves, and could be good or bad, right or wrong, without reference to man and his psycho-physiological nature. This attitude has affected the progress and understanding of architecture as sub-zero cold affects the grease of a car, as a wire fence affects poultry, and as a blindfold affects the eyes. When Minkowski and Einstein restated the postulates of physics and mathematics *to include man*, the grease became a lubricant, the fence had open gates, and the blindfolds fell off. While this is rather an involved figure, perhaps it explains the large crop of scientific "geniuses" we have since produced. It is to be hoped that an extension of the same principles to questions of architecture will have a similarly invigorating and re-

leasing effect, not only upon architects but upon all mankind (which, willy-nilly, is for the most part under constant exposure to architecture).

This book, then, is an inquiry into the psycho-physiological considerations involved in architecture. The subject is vast, and although I have spent some eight years in preparing the material, it is no more than an introduction, an entering wedge, a beginning. But if I have succeeded in stating some of the basic postulates, formulations, and principles adequately enough to serve as a foundation for further work, I shall consider my labor well spent.

In line with this, it will be found that some of what I have to say will seem simple and obvious (at least I hope so) particularly in the opening pages, where it is my purpose merely to establish a few fundamental points upon which to build later. The far-reaching and revolutionary character of the conclusions reached in the study as a whole will, however, become apparent upon reflection.

I have chosen (human behavior in action!) to use the technique of General Semantics* in the study, find-

---

* "General Semantics turned out to be an empirical natural science of non-elementalistic evaluation, which takes into account the living individual, not divorcing him from his reactions altogether, nor from his neuro-linguistic and neuro-semantic environments, but allocating him in a plenum of some values, no matter what." (p. viii) "Unfortunately our educational systems are unaware of, or even negativistic toward, such *neuro*-semantic and *neuro*-linguistic issues." "Modern scientific developments show that what we label 'objects' or 'objective' are mere nervous constructs inside of our skulls which our nervous systems have abstracted electro-colloidally from the actual world of electronic processes on the sub-microscopic level. And so we have to face a complete de-

ing it highly appropriate for dealing with the many doctrinal and linguistic aspects of architecture. In doing so I have had to face certain difficulties. It would be impossible, for instance, to include in the text the full semantic processes I used, for such inclusion would necessarily entail explanations of neuro-linguistic and neuro-semantic responses, such formulations as "$\dfrac{\text{over}}{\text{under}}$ definition," etc., all of which would, in sheer bulk, outweigh the architectural material. Also it would be most fraudulent of me to entice a reader with the promise of saying something about architecture, in which he is presumably interested, only to plunge him into a heavy volume on semantics, concerning which I have no reason to believe he cares a hoot, and about which, if he *is* interested, he could readily learn from much more qualified writers.

parture from two-valued, 'objective' orientations to *general, infinite-valued, process orientations. . . .*" In calling the submicroscopic world the "actual" one, Korzybski is making what appears to me to be an unwarranted choice. All levels are equally "actual" or "illusory" if one accepts Korzybski's own neuro-perceptual "process orientation." Nevertheless, the point he makes relates very closely to my effort to analyze architecture as a group of processes taking place *within* the minds of the designers and observers and therefore not understandable in any totally objective sense.

"I must stress that I give no panaceas, but experience shows that when the methods of general semantics are *applied,* the results are usually beneficial, whether in business, management, etc., medicine, law, education on all levels, or personal inter-relationships, be they in family, national, or international fields. . . . The prevalent and constantly increasing general deterioration of human values is an unavoidable consequence of the crippling misuse of *neuro*-linguistic and *neuro*-semantic mechanisms." Alfred H. Korzybski, *Science and Sanity.*

For this and other reasons, I have kept the semantic processes largely out of the text and confined myself to the architectural conclusions which that process has made possible. Such semantic references as I have, of necessity, had to make, are over-simplified to a shameful degree, and I herewith apologize humbly to all serious semanticists for taking such unwarranted liberties.

Nevertheless, not to be too cavalier with an important field of study, I have indicated, at appropriate points (through footnotes and references) *where* in General Semantics I made my principal points of entry into the method. Should a reader be interested in reconstructing the process, these will, I trust, serve as adequate clues. The semantics text of which I made the greatest use was *Science and Sanity,* Alfred Korzybski's monumental work upon which most other inquiries into semantics have been based. To him and to numerous other writers of less inclusive but more concentrated intention, I owe a debt of gratitude for introducing me to the method used in the present study.

I also wish to acknowledge my indebtedness to my friend and colleague, Professor Talbot F. Hamlin, for reading and criticizing the manuscript, and to Dean Leopold Arnaud, whose wise guidance and encouragement led to both the inception and the completion of the work.

The financial problems connected with the actual execution of the book were solved through the grant (1951–52) of the Langley Scholarship of the American Institute of Architects, whose support made it possible.

E. R.

New York, June 1954

Architecturally
Speaking

Architecture

Einstein, in thus analyzing what is involved in making a judgment of simultaneity, and in seizing on the act of the observer as the essence of the situation, is actually adopting a new point of view as to what the concepts of physics should be. . . .
Percy W. Bridgman, *The Logic of Modern Physics*

Architecture

ARCHITECTURE INVOLVES MANY SPE-
cific considerations—dimensions, weights, stresses, etc.
—about which there is seldom room for disagreement.
If any question arises concerning, say, the length of a
certain corridor or the height of a certain building, it is
a simple matter to measure it or to read the size off a
scale drawing. We do not sit up nights arguing over
the weight of a cubic foot of concrete or the crushing
strength of brick. We put it to the test. We use, in short,
the operational approach.

But architecture also includes numerous intangibles
—unity, rhythm, scale, grandeur, to mention only a
few. Concerning these there is plenty of room for disagreement; so much, in fact, that heads have rolled because of them.* And since there is no way of going out
and measuring unity or grandeur, the disagreements are
seldom resolved but continue to grow in both magni-
tude and intensity until they finally achieve the re-
spectable status of Schools of Thought.

A certain rather jolly field of study called *semantics*
has developed a technique for resolving differences in-

* The Emperor Hadrian of Rome in the second century A.D.
ordered the execution of Apollodorus of Damascus, an architect
who disagreed with the Emperor over the esthetics of a proposed temple.

3

volving intangibles. It is known as "find the referent." In other words, find the specific thing or things to which the intangible under discussion refers.*

The device employed in this fascinating game is the "abstraction ladder." A series of terms is set in vertical order, leading from the intangible (abstraction) at the top to the specific thing (referent) at the bottom. While this process is not guaranteed to settle all disputes, it will most certainly do a great deal toward clarifying the issue and putting a halt to endless quantities of random sniping.

Let us say, for example, that A and B disagree about the nature of happiness. After coming almost to blows, each constructs an "abstraction ladder." A's ladder looks like this:

> Happiness
> Love
> Woman
> Sweetheart
> Ethel

B's ladder, it turns out, reads somewhat differently:

> Happiness
> Fun
> Sport
> Fishing
> Trout

A is understandably resentful over any comparisons be-

* The term *semantics* ordinarily refers to the study of meanings and significances in verbal expressions. But *General Semantics* is now understood as the name for a new structural approach in which man is considered as a whole; his perceptions, interpretations, knowledge, intellectual and emotional reactions, and bodily functions are treated as inseparable phases of a total psycho-physiological process.

4

tween a fish and his beloved, and B fails to see how anyone could waste time on a quarry that puts up so little fight. C, who has been sitting by, is a married man. His idea of happiness involves both his wife and fish, and his abstraction ladder is consequently more complicated. (What about Ethel's ladder? Or the trout's?)*

* The specific referent at the foot of the ladder can just as well be an action as an object, or a combination of the two, as in "looking at architecture," which to those so inclined is the referent for "happiness." Or, in a more general application, the ladder might be set up this way:

> Happiness
> Self-transcendence
> Breadth-of-life sense
> Rapport with universe
> Watching the ocean

Here the act of "watching," combined with the object watched, "ocean," make up the referent. The subjective reactions, and the reactions to the reactions, lead to the concluding abstraction "happiness."

5

At any rate, it should become clear to Messrs. A and B that although they might discuss the relative charms of Ethel and trout, there is very little point to their arguing about happiness. Their referents for the abstraction "happiness" being different, they are not talking about the same thing at all.

Unfortunately, most people never bother to find the referents for the abstractions they use. If pressed to say what they mean by one abstraction, they will often answer with another. This process sometimes results in elegant language but seldom in any clarification.

Take the term "architecture" itself. Even men who devote their whole lives to architecture find it hard to say just what they mean by the word.

X will say it means "the art and science of building." Of course, both "art" and "science" are abstractions of a high order, having to do with processes in which the rational and intuitive faculties are used in widely varying and unmeasurable proportions. One could argue interminably over what one means by "art" as distinct from "science,"* let alone how much of each is involved in "architecture." Y prefers Sir Henry Wotten's phrase, "commodity, firmness and delight." Since each of these would describe Marilyn Monroe just as aptly as the Parthenon, the phrase is not much help in arriving at a definition of architecture. Goethe's poetic expression, "frozen music," which Z swears by, has an intriguing sound

* ". . . mathematicians have an intuitive predilection for selecting their terms and pursuing their line of enquiry among *possible meanings* . . . the feeling which directs the selection of material which is . . . interesting and important is akin to the artistic sense, but, unfortunately . . . has been neglected by 'psychologists.' " Alfred H. Korzybski, *Science and Sanity.*

but a disappointing lack of substance, for music at a standstill has neither melody, rhythm, nor harmonic sequence. It is just as difficult to grasp an image of such music as to accept architecture without theme, pattern, or sequence.

What, then, is architecture? Or rather, what *specific* referents can we find for it?

I remember as a small child being taken to some public building by my father. There, on one of the walls, was a great mural painting depicting a muscular giant, almost nude, holding a cluster of ships in one hand and some trucks in the other. Airplanes buzzed around his head, and a long train wound its way between his outsize feet.

"Who is that?" I asked, clutching at my father's leg.

"Transportation," he replied. And even to this day I get curious mental pictures when I read in the paper that Transportation Is Tied Up, or Transportation Increases 50%. The effect of this kind of personification is to make it hard to realize the extremely simple fact that the abstraction "transportation" has vehicles, drivers, cargo, and passengers for its referents. That's all. There is no giant, clothed or otherwise.

Similarly, "architecture" consists of architects, buildings, and people. There is no gracious lady in classic robes, holding aloft a pair of dividers and a triangle, however thrilling such an image may seem. And there is definitely not so much as a single chip of frozen music.

Insofar as the architect is concerned, architecture is above all a *creative process*. He has an idea in his mind, an effect, an emotion, let us say, which he wishes to express in terms of structure. His intention of going

8

beyond mere utility to express something of greater human meaning is architecture, *to him,* regardless of the success or failure of his actual accomplishment. To the architect, in short, architecture is a subjective matter dependent upon his purpose. The element of *purpose,* therefore, must find its place in our definition of architecture.

The observer (people-in-general) is uninformed as to the architect's purpose. He looks at a building, and an image falls upon the retina of his eye by a process as mechanical as photography. This image has no meaning to him until his mind has interpreted it and his emotions have responded to it. Of course, such interpretive and emotional responses are totally dependent upon his personal sensitivity and the degree of his training. The observer's consciousness of architecture, in other words, is as much a subjective matter as the architect's purpose. There is no architecture for the observer, except insofar as he is aware of it. *Awareness,* then, is the second element in our definition.

Thus far we have been speaking of matters existing either in the mind of the architect or the mind of the observer. What of the structure itself? Surely the structure, to be architecture, must contain some characteristics that have an objective reality other than dimension and weight. Here we are on softer ground. We can say no more than that the structure must be composed of shapes, colors, textures, lights, and darks—physical elements, in short, which are *capable* of evoking the emotional awareness already referred to as the observer's response and *capable* of expressing the purpose of the architect. We must always come back to the observer and the architect, as representatives of the human species, because architecture exists only for humans. We do not expect a dog to be stirred by the majesty of the Pantheon or the tracery of Rheims. Clearly, therefore, when we attempt to define the objective characteristics of architecture we are doing nothing more than approaching human subjectivity from another angle.

Architecture can thus be understood in three ways —three levels, if you like. One, the creative intention of the designer; two, the potential evocativity of the structure itself; and three, the response of the observer.

Usually when people disagree over whether or not a certain building is architecture, their differences of opinion lie in each of them having taken only one of the three possible views of the matter. One may be attacking or defending the intention of the designer, another may be revealing his own sensitivity—or lack of it— while yet a third may be attempting to analyze the building in accordance with some esoteric formula of proportions.

The abstraction "architecture," tracked down to its referents, becomes a trio of emotions—emotion intended, emotion inherent, and emotion evoked. The common element is emotion, and if one must use a single term to define architecture, that is it. Architecture is emotion. If the emotion is mild, so is the architecture. If the emotion is great, the architecture is great. If there is no emotion, there is no architecture; there is only building.

I am blandly using the word "emotion" here as though it were a term with a single, well-accepted meaning. Since it is very far from being such, I must specify not its "true meaning," for there is no such thing, but the sense in which I mean to apply it.

Actually, the complex neural reactions and inter-reactions that go on within us can no more be separated into parts labelled "intellect" and "emotion," than "space" can be separated from "time," or "body" from "mind." These splits, which are possible only under the Aristotelian structure of our language, have already been discarded by modern medicine and physics.

But granting that "emotion" and "intellect" are inseparable, there are still neural activities which are more thalamic than cortical, or more cortical than thalamic. They are more (or less) in the lower, automatic areas of the brain or more (or less) in the upper, cortical layers, in which association and reasoning take place. It is in this sense that I use the word "emotion"; "feelings," "moods," "states of mind," etc., fall into this category.

It is significant, in view of many of the points to be made in successive chapters, that these "feelings" deal almost exclusively with the individual's relation to his world, which is not surprising when one considers that matters such as fear, safety, and so forth are among the most fundamental and ancient concerns of all living creatures.

In relation to specific buildings, examples of architecture, we feel ourselves to be small (a sense of awe); exalted (a sense of belonging to something larger than ourselves); protected (a sense of shelter); dominated (a sense of the power of authority); uplifted (a sense of the mystery of God). In all these cases, and many others that come easily to mind, the thing to note is that the observer asks himself, "What is this building to me?" or rather, "What am I to it?" Large? Small? Weak? Strong? Protected? Exposed? Threatened? Scorned? Gratified?

The basic desires and fears of the observer as touched and activated by architecture are the "emotions" to which I refer. They are the essence of architecture, the core of the meaning of architecture, on the lowest primitive levels of survival-motives no less than on the loftiest transcendent aspirations of which we are capable.

Style

The little word is has its tragedies; it marries and identifies things with the greatest innocence; and yet no two
are ever identical, and if therein lies the charm of wed-
ding them and calling them one, therein too lies the
danger. Whenever I use the word is, except in sheer
tautology, I deeply misuse it; and when I discover my
error, the world seems to fall asunder and the members
of my family no longer know one another.

George Santayana, *Scepticism and Animal Faith*

Style

THE WORD "STYLE" IS AN ABSTRACTION
of a particularly high order in that it concerns the manner in which things are done. Manner, in turn, is itself an intangible quantity, depending upon the perception, interpretation, and recognition by an observer of the specific items which identify it. Style can exist, therefore, only insofar as our eyes and minds are trained to select and appreciate similarities and differences of manner.*

The manner of each individual is unique. Each man drives a car, dances a rhumba, cooks an egg, makes love, and designs buildings in his own individual way because he is individually different from all other men. As a matter of fact, aside from his name and his physical being, it is his personal manner or *style* of thinking and acting that makes him the individual he is. It is frequently said that the imprint of his personality shows

* "Since no two events are identical, every atom, molecule, organism, personality, and society is an emergent and, at least to some extent, a novelty. And these emergents are concatenated in such a way as to form vast ramifying systems, only certain ideal sections of which seem to have elicited the attention of philosophers, owing to their avowedly anthropocentric and anthropodoxic interests." William Morton Wheeler, Proceedings of Sixth International Congress of Philosophers, Harvard.

15

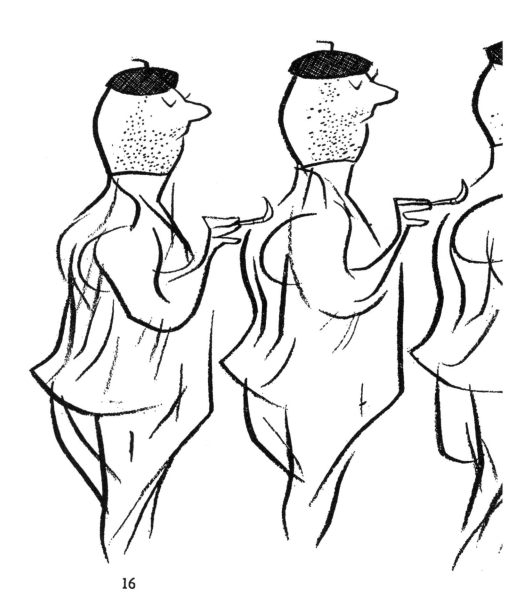

17

in a man's every word and deed, but the deeper truth may well be that the sum of words and deeds *is* the personality. At any rate, this is a point of view to which certain schools of psychology subscribe.

If the style of an artist—painter, sculptor, musician, architect—is the reflection or manifestation of his personality, which is my contention, then clearly his style can be different from that of other men only inasmuch as and to the degree that his personality differs from that of others. It is perhaps an unconscious recognition of this fact that makes so many striving artists work so hard at being "characters." Somehow they feel that if only they can make themselves peculiar enough, their art will achieve style. Unfortunately too many of them choose the same way (manner, style) of being peculiar, and in their desperate efforts towards uniqueness succeed in attaining only uniformity.

The greatest artist, the one with the most individual style, is the loneliest of men. In fact, his personality (style, manner) is so far removed from the average of his period that frequently he is unrecognized and unrewarded until long after his death. We can only hope that somewhere in the personality-style-manner complex that makes up his being there is also an element that might be called soul, possessed of both immortality and consciousness. There may then be some comfort in being able to sit on a cloud, reading the latest critical praises, and murmuring to one's angelic companions, "Naturally. I knew it all along."

The mediocre personality, the man who approaches being the average product of his culture, can never produce work that is more than mediocre. You have only to look at three-fourths of contemporary architec-

18

tural work to realize that it might have been designed by any of three-fourths of contemporary architects. Let me repeat, if we accept *style* as being an expression of personality, then there is no way for a mediocre personality to have anything but a mediocre style. The sharply individualistic style can come only from the sharply individual creator. It is probably for this reason that those few men whose styles are strongly personal are such controversial figures. The crowd either hates or adores the outsider; sometimes it does both at the same time.

I do not mean to imply that a median personality is doomed forever to mediocrity. It is a first principle of life that we are all capable of growth and change, a principle without which all hope and effort would be truly futile.

The concept of "style" may also be approached historically. Although it is true that each individual is different from all others and has a style all his own, it is also true that we are all more or less products of the same period and culture, if we are contemporaries. Thus, all men who are living now, in this culture, drive cars, dance the rhumba, cook eggs, and make love in a *similar* way (manner, style).

This similarity, *distinguishable from the similarities of other periods and cultures,* constitutes the historical style of our period. A style name is no more than a shorthand statement symbolizing those similarities in the works of one period that are different from the similarities of another period. For example, the word Gothic, as spoken architecturally, refers to all those resemblances among buildings of that style that are different from the resemblances among Romanesque

19

20

buildings, say, or buildings bearing any other style label.

In this sense the style of contemporary architecture must be understood to include such things as veneered half-timbered Olde Englishe apartment houses just as well as cantilevered floor slabs and curtain walls of glass. The fact that you can look at a "Norman" or "Tudor" residence in Westchester and recognize it as an expression of contemporary culture is sufficient proof. Never mind whether or not you approve of this aspect of our culture—there are other aspects even more doubtful—your instant ability to state almost the exact year in which it was built means that it is no more Norman or Tudor than you are. It is a house in the Contemporary Style. It remains for the historian of the future to give our style a proper name. Neo-Juke Box? Syntho-Classic? Meanwhile we shall have to be content with a working title—Contemporary.

Being as close to the work as we are, we are more aware of differences than similarities. But this same historian of the future will be conscious, in all our buildings, of similarities which we take so much for granted that we hardly see them—in workmanship, in materials, in scale, in patterns of living, standards of amenity—all of which will make very clear to him our stylistic brotherhood.

There is still another sense in which the word "style" is used—as a synonym for elegance, dash, conviction, and spirit in the execution of a design. When used this way, style does not refer either to the historic period of the work or to the personality of the designer, but rather to one of the qualities or characteristics that the work possesses. You say, "That building has lots of

21

style," although it may be a building in the Georgian Style, in which you recognize the personal style of Architect So-and-so.

To sum up, the abstraction "style" may be analyzed on three levels: as a reflection of the designer's individual personality, as an identification of a period and culture, and as a quality of execution in the work itself. Perhaps the highest stylistic achievement occurs when a highly developed and exceptional individual expresses the essence of his cultural period with the maximum of technical skill. Then you have STYLE at all three levels, and the least we can do is to show our respect by capitalizing it.

Unity

. . . *if we use the word intelligence as a synonym for mental activity, as is often done, we must differentiate between the primitive forms of sensory intelligence, with their ill-developed symbolism beyond which backward children cannot advance . . . and the forms of verbal intelligence created by social education, abstract and conceptual forms.*

—Henri Piéron, *Thought and the Brain*

Unity

To EXPLORE THE CONCEPT OF "UNITY" calls for considerable stubbornness, as well as a willingness to endure the anger of your friends. For if you ask someone, "What is unity?" the chances are he will purse his lips pedantically and give you some such answer as this:

"Unity, ahem, unity is that indispensable element of any composition which gives coherence to the parts and integrity to the whole."

"Gosh," you say, admiringly. "That sounds swell. But what *is* unity?"

"I've told you that!" says your friend. "You've got to have it, that's all!"

"All right," you say, "I don't mind having it. But what is it?"

At this point your friend makes a rude remark and leaves, perhaps first flinging an inkwell at your head if he knows you well enough.

Aside from the resulting lump, you are still left with your question. What is unity?

The word "unity" means oneness. Of course, no actual oneness exists, unless you get down to the single-cell organism or the atom and even that (as has recently been brought to our attention) can be split into parts.

When we speak of unity we do not mean this kind of oneness. We are referring to the putting-together of things, the composing of things, the combining of things into a group to which we can then attribute the quality of oneness. The key word here is the word *attribute*. We begin our analysis of unity, therefore, with the recognition that it does not exist *in* the composition. It is something which we *attribute* to it.

Into my field of vision there strolls a creature who consists of a combination of parts. He has four feet, one torso, one tail, two eyes, two ears and one nose. I accept this combination of parts as a dog because I am familiar with the concept "dog." I know what a dog is, and I know what parts a dog has (even if I haven't listed them all).

If I should see a dog with two tails, I would sense a violation of my concept "dog." I would be inclined to shut one eye, hold my hand in such a position as to block out the extra tail, and say, "This design would have increased unity if that element were removed." All I am saying, of course, is that a second tail to a dog does not fit my experience of dogs.

Here is a table. It has a rectangular, flat surface, four uprights, an apron along each of its sides. We accept this combination of parts as having unity because it conforms to an idea we have of what a table is.

Again, we look at a cathedral. We know what takes place in a cathedral; we know the rituals, what the crossing is for, the apse, the nave, the chapels. We recognize the combination of parts and the functions which they represent, so we accept the unity that exists in putting them together. If from one of the towers a cantilevered hot dog stand jutted forth, we

26

would fail to understand its presence in this combination of parts. To put it gently, it would be an extraneous element, detracting from unity.

Our first principle of unity, therefore, is a clear understanding of the nature and function of a composition, be it a building, an animal, or a gadget. To accept a composition as having *unity*, one must know and recognize the functions of the parts and the rightness of putting them together to serve the function of the whole. Without such understanding, we do not *attribute* unity, and so, for us at any rate, unity does not exist.

Of course, our understanding is subject to change as we learn new things. For example, a wagon forms a composition which lacks unity unless there is a horse in front of it. But if you put a hood at its front, and rubber tires on its wheels, your concept of it changes. It is no longer a wagon; it is an automobile and has full unity without a horse, although it takes some time for certain people to accept such a new concept, as illustrated by the cries of "Git a horse!" which followed motorists for a good many years during the early days of the motor car.

Context also has a profound effect upon our concepts and acceptance of unity. Place this same auto in motion, on a highway, and it will look rather odd without a driver.

What about the driver without the car? Does he lack unity? No, because the human being on his own two feet is still conceivable as an independent *organism*, and is in fact frequently thus seen, particularly indoors or in special outdoor areas such as golf courses. However, in a good many communities where the automotive culture is in a high stage of development to go anywhere without your Buick is to be practically naked.

Concepts and contexts are as varied and complex as modern life. That is why we have so many building types, so many kinds of equipment, so many kinds of art. Our heads are crowded with ideas and associations in a way that may be likened to a random card index file, voluminous and untidy, but cross referenced way down into the subconscious. When we look at any object at all, we go through a process very much like searching through the file for a card which matches what we see. If we come up with a card that reads "dog," or "table," or "cathedral" and it fits what is before our eyes, we are pleased and accept the dog, the table, or the cathedral as having unity. If the card matches in all but one respect, say, then we complain of the odd element as a violation of unity. If we cannot find a card at all, we are annoyed and tend to sneer or shrug and turn away.

Sometimes we fail to find a card, not because the expression of the design is unclear but because of a lack in our own experience; we have not yet filled out and filed such a card. For example, a man who has seen very few "modern" houses is confronted with a Le Corbusier specimen. He searches frantically through his file but finds nothing that fits. The only card he comes up with is one marked Small Industry. Rather than admit his own lack, he thereupon insists that what he is looking at is a pickle factory. And of course, it has no unity, for where are the pickle vats?

In the case of abstract painting or sculpture, the card index search takes place at a level of subconscious association. Forms, colors, patterns which one does not identify in any representational sense suggest not objects or concepts but the emotions associated with them. To respond readily at this level requires considerable sensitivity, willingness, and training. It takes practice to turn off the conscious, verbal faculties deliberately and allow delicate combinations of feeling to float up to the surface of perception. That is why one sees so many bemused faces at exhibitions of modern art. And that is also why those people who have neither the sensitivity, the willingness, nor the training to go through this process are so contemptuous of all modern art and so sure that it consists entirely of charlatanry. Which is not to say that there is no fakery at all in the modern art world. Even a die-hard academician can be partially right!*

In the case of buildings, the recognition of concepts is tied up closely with expression of function. The purpose which a structure serves must be clearly stated in its design before the observer's eye can light up with the glow that says, "I know! That's a bank." Or a school, a church, a bus terminal. Otherwise, he will be forced to fumble through his file at random; his chances of achieving any perception of unity will be slim indeed.

In stylistically traditional architecture the expression of function or purpose is relatively easy, for we are

* "Vancouver, B. C., Feb. 3 (1952). A 17-year-old artist admitted today that an abstract painting a Toronto art gallery had placed on exhibition was only an old piece of cardboard on which commercial painters had cleaned their brushes. . . . Nealess . . . had . . . sent it to Toronto under the title, "Melancholia in the Swamp." United Press, *The New York Times*, Feb. 6, 1952.

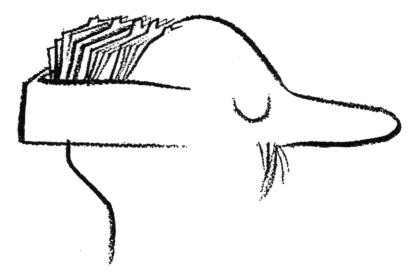

dealing with well-established vocabularies of form and well-known building types. It is not difficult to design a "Gothic" chapel and have it recognized as such. It might as well bear a sign* stating just what it is. But when we discard established forms, when we "go mod-

* "In the rough, a symbol is defined as a sign which stands for something. Any sign is not necessarily a symbol. If it stands for something, it becomes a symbol for this something. If it does not stand for something, then it becomes not a symbol *but* a meaningless sign. This applies to words just as it does to bank cheques. If one has a zero balance in the bank but still has a cheque-book and issues a check, he issues a sign but not a symbol because it does not stand for anything. The penalty for such use of these particular signs as symbols is usually jailing. This analogy applies to the oral noises we make, which occasionally become symbols and at other times do not; as yet, no penalty is exacted for such a fraud." Alfred H. Korzybski, *Science and Sanity.*

The analogy also applies to architecture; the penalty for the misuse of signs is affective failure.

30

ern," the road becomes rougher. To the unpracticed eye all "modern" buildings look alike, an endless sequence of grim planes and intersections; the observer cannot distinguish one building type from another, cannot identify the functions and purposes, and hence is unable to find an index card in his concept file against which to check for unity. This is not always the fault of the unpracticed eye. Many architects are unfortunately unaware of the *absolute necessity* of making contact with the observer's conceptual equipment if unity (functional expression and recognition) is to be achieved. I do not mean to suggest that we should stick to stylistically traditional forms. I merely wish to point out, as emphatically as I can, that the fresh forms we use must be as easily read and as easily understood as the old. It is in this task of finding new methods of expression that the most serious challenge to the creative imagination of the modern architect lies.

As a matter of fact, we could not stay with traditional expressions even if we wanted to. There is no traditional expression for a new building type, a type arising out of a new social need. The drive-in restaurant, the airport buildings, the combination hotel-shopping-theatre-parking project—are there any traditional expressions for these? Of course, some architects try to cloak these new functions by wrapping them in a traditional disguise, in an effort as desperate and as futile as that of the benighted soul who plops a radio-phonograph-TV combination into a Chippendale cabinet.

No matter how well it is designed, a radio-phonograph-TV set cannot possibly have unity to a person from some distant jungle who has never heard of wireless transmission or electrical amplification. To such a person the set would seem to be a random collection of elements. A few knobs, dials, or screens more or less would make no difference to him. Only the eye which understands the *nature* and *function* of the elements is capable of perceiving unity or the lack of it.

With this last illustration, we are ready to sum up our analysis of unity as it applies to architectural design. The whole thing, as we have seen, hinges upon the ability of the architect to form a clear concept of his project in human and social terms before he sets pencil to paper. Then throughout the process of designing he must hold to that concept unwaveringly, ruthlessly eliminating anything and everything that contradicts it, developing and emphasizing everything that expresses it. If this turns out to be impossible, something is wrong with his concept, and he had better go back and form a new one. No amount of juggling with proportions, fiddling with scale, or imposing of continuous overhangs will bring unity to a design which is conceptually inconsistent. Clarity of concept is the inescapable basis for unity.

It may be argued that this statement is arbitrary in its exclusion of such matters as easily apprehended shapes—spheres, triangles, etc.—which permit the eye a simple comprehension of unity in pure form; it is my contention that there is no such thing as unity in pure form; to the mind ignorant of the concepts, the shapes have no meaning. As a *device for facilitating conceptual expression* in buildings, the use of readily understood forms has great value, however, which must not be underestimated.

I submit, therefore, that the selection of particular

32

shapes is a question of *device*, to be ranked with other architectural devices such as scale, color, harmony, ornament, rhythm, dominance, subordination, etc., which are used to enhance conceptual unity but which in themselves *are not* the unity. The unity is in the concept.

If the conceptual approach to "unity" is accepted, it becomes clear that the architect of today must be well abreast of current thought. How can he design even a jail, say, if he is not up on present day ideas about penology? Is a jail a place where evil people are punished? Is it a storehouse for the human refuse of society? Is it a sort of hospital where sick people are cared for so that they may be returned to normal life? Without a clear opinion based upon thought and study the architect cannot so much as begin to form the basic concept upon which the unity of his design will depend. It is not enough to know *how* to build. One must first know *what* one is building.

What assurance is there that the observer's concepts are as developed as the architect's? What reason is there to believe that he, too, is *au courant* with the latest and most advanced ideas of his society? The answer is, none. But if the architect is an average man, the chances are that his concepts will match those of the average observer. If he is in the forefront of modern thought, or even ahead of it, he will be looked up to as a genius (if his public relations are good) or down upon as a wild-eyed crackpot (if they're not so good). People have card indices for "genius" and "crackpot" too.

Scale

'Near' is a place to which I can get quickly on my feet, not a place to which the train or the air-ship will take me quickly. 'Far' is a place to which I cannot get quickly on my feet. . . . Man is the measure. That was my first lesson. Man's feet are the measure for distance, his hands are the measure for ownership, his body is the measure for all that is lovable and desirable and strong.

E. M. Forster, *Collected Tales*

Scale

IT IS NECESSARY TO PAUSE HERE FOR a moment and point out that in the first two chapters, those dealing with the terms "architecture" and "style," we were attempting to define areas of meaning; we were tracking abstractions down to their referents. We were not concerned particularly with success or degree of accomplishment in architectural expression. Our primary interest was to *define* rather than to judge. Thus we touched only very lightly on questions of good or bad architecture, successful or unsuccessful stylistic expression.

With the chapter on "unity" we were no longer merely defining; we were setting up critical standards, for we were saying that unity is a quality that is indispensable to good architecture, that without it the architecture is bad. The moment we do this we are departing from the process of semantic analysis and entering the field of criticism, also known as preaching. This I freely admit, along with the existence of those inevitable elements of bias which can always be found in criticism. As a matter of fact, bias needs no defense. I have no respect for the words of someone who has no opinions, and what is bias but the opinion of someone else?

In this regard I shall say only one thing more. As we continue to discuss those aspects of architecture whose treatment makes it "good" or "bad," I shall necessarily expose my own bias. If the reader's prejudices happen to coincide with mine, he will probably not notice the bias at all. But if he disagrees with me, I beg him to imagine my prejudices deleted and his own substituted. The semantic or rational elements of our analysis will be unaffected, argument will be avoided, and everyone will be happy.

"Proper" scale, then, along with unity, is considered a desirable quality in architecture. In fact, as I have already pointed out, "good" scale is one of the devices used to achieve unity. I have put the words "proper" and "good" in quotes because at this point, in advance of analysis, we have not yet decided what proper and good scale is. At the moment we know only that we want it.

A scale is a measuring instrument, marked off in centimeters, inches, pounds, or whatever the units to be measured happen to be. A scale drawing is one in which one dimension is represented by another in a fixed relationship. Thus one foot of a real structure may be represented by one quarter of an inch on a drawing. When you look at the drawing, you *see* one quarter of an inch but you *think* one foot because you have accepted the relationship. If you have not been informed about the relationship (¼″ equals 1′) and have no way of deducing it, you still see the dimensions drawn on the paper but you do not know what dimensions to think. There is no scale.

When you look at an actual building, you are still not seeing real dimensions. You see an image on your retina cast there through the lens of your eye. This image will vary in size depending upon your distance from the structure. Between the image and the reality there is a scale relationship. You *see* the dimensions of the image, but you *think* the dimensions of the building. In other words, whether you are looking at a drawing of a building or at the building itself, you are always looking at a scale picture. The sizes in the picture represent the true sizes of the building, which you interpret by knowing or deducing the scale of the picture.

On paper, you know the scale. It says so, right there on the drawing: ¼″ equals 1′, or 1½″ equals 1′, or what have you. Moreover, once drawn, the scale does not change. Except for possible shrinkage in the paper, ¼″ will always represent one foot. But the scale relationship between a real structure and the image in your eye is constantly changing as you move towards, around, into, or away from the building. The eye must perform a continuous task of deduction and interpretation, most of it automatic and instantaneous. It is a delicate business, subject to easy error.

A writer of the nineteenth century tells the story of a man seated in the library of his house on the bank of a river. He had been reading about ancient legends, when he happened to glance up and out the window. There, across the river, ascending a hill, was the largest and most horrendous dragon ever conceived in fable or song. Trembling but brave, our man approached the window for a better look, when suddenly he realized (somewhat to his relief, I imagine) that the dragon across the river was only an insect on his window pane.

In the language of our present analysis, this was an

error of scale interpretation. Actually, the wonder is not that we make such errors but that we make so few of them. When you consider that the Empire State Building, seen from Long Island, is no bigger than your little finger held at arm's length, but from close by, it overflows your field of vision, you gain new respect for the flexibility of your powers of scale interpretation.

I repeatedly use the phrase "scale interpretation" because by now it should be clear that the abstraction "good scale" has as its referent, "scale that is correctly interpreted" while the abstraction "bad scale" boils down to "scale that is erroneously interpreted." No building is ever "out of scale" (a misleading phrase). Every building is actually the size that it is, and the image of it on your retina is as accurate as your vision allows. It is in the process of interpretation that the trouble, if any, arises. If the architect has given you inadequate or misleading scale clues, if he has overestimated your perceptiveness or underestimated your laziness, you fail to make a successful scale interpretation. If you are trained in the vocabulary of architecture, you say the building is "out of scale." If you are untrained, you say nothing. You just walk away with a vague sense of dissatisfaction.

Why the dissatisfaction, vague or otherwise? Why should we care if our scale interpretations are correct or not? Does it make any difference to us if we think the Empire State Building is 500 feet or 1000 feet high? Its proportions, its silhouette will still be the same, and we can enjoy it just as much (if we enjoy it at all).

Psychologists tell us that what they mean by a "sense

40

of security" is an acceptance by the individual of his relationship with his environment. This does not necessarily mean approval—he may want to change it—but he knows what his environment is and how he stands with regard to it. If he doesn't know what it is, he cannot tell how he stands. This frightens him, and he then suffers from "insecurity." His fear can range from panic (Abbott and Costello in a haunted house) down to a mild sensation of displeasure ("That building is out of scale"). In every case the individual feels that he does not quite know how he stands in relation to his world. Abbott and Costello do not know what is making that fearsome noise; our architectural observer does not know how to interpret the size of this building.

The perception—or, rather, estimate—of size is also tied up, as we have pointed out, with comprehension of distance. Just as you cannot tell how large the dragon is or how tall the Empire State Building is unless you know how far away from it you are, you cannot tell how far away from something you are without some clues—perspective lines, intervening elements, or best of all, a definite knowledge of the size of the object being regarded. Imagine, for example, a flat desert, nothing but sand from horizon to horizon. Suddenly a man appears. Instantly, you can judge his distance from you because you know the size of a man. But cactus varies so much in size, that if you caught sight of a cactus plant instead of a man, its size would give you no clue as to its distance, nor would its distance help you guess its size. This last example is not altogether true—you can get a rough idea of distance by relating the object to the horizon and also by the focussing angle tension in your eye muscles—but it is substantially true.

In architecture, then, the problem of scale is that of *facilitating the orientation of the observer with regard to the structure*. It is not merely a matter of making sizes and distances apparent. They must be made apparent *easily* and *agreeably*. In his emotional responses, your observer is a delicate, readily upset bird. Nor does he feel that his whole existence depends upon his liking a given building. If his sense of security (relationship to the structure, in this case) is at all disturbed, even to the very slightest degree, that is the end of it for him. That is why scale is of such great importance.*

How do you soothe this poor, sensitive fellow? Well, the simplest method is to show him things whose size he knows very well. These, in general, are the things with which he has had long and close contact. Railings, for example. He knows the size of railings intimately, because he has walked beside them innumerable times. He knows just how far he bends his arm to put his hand on them, and just where on his hip he would feel the pressure should he lean on them. He knows stairs, too, from his first disastrous encounters with them in his infancy. He is familiar with doors and windows, particularly casements and hung sash which he has operated. He is also familiar

---

* "It must be realized that for the 'normal' working of the nervous system we must have proper blood circulation, which may be affected by the *tension* of the blood vessels, and is also connected with emotional *tension* . . . which involves hidden fears, anxieties, uncertainties, frustrations, etc., and through the nervous mechanism of projection color harmfully our attitudes toward the world and life in general." Alfred H. Korzybski, *Science and Sanity*.

with units of construction which he has handled, such as brick.*

Of course, if you persist in using a vocabulary of elements with which people have long been familiar, you are by way of being a "traditionalist," which in some circles comes close to being a dirty word. But I submit to you that the whole process of scale interpretation is one in which the eye seeks things of familiar size. You *must* give your observer things that he knows, no matter how much it hurts your advanced soul.

That is why scale problems are so hard to solve in "modern" architecture and why they so frequently fail of solution. When you design a building of simple concrete planes, no cornices, flush doors (trimless, of course), and strip windows, there is not much with which to show scale—the glass panes, perhaps, and a step or two at the door. Those modern architects who have rediscovered ornament and natural materials are having more success with scale than their purist prophets. I do not mean to say that ornament or the materials of which I speak—stone, brick, wood, tile—need to be used in a traditional manner. Their mere *existence* in a design often turns the scale trick.

* In this connection it is important to point out the close relation, neurologically, between "seeing" and "doing." In using a building we actually touch the hand rails, step upon the stairs, etc., and it is through these tactile contacts that our experiences are formed. But the tactile contacts are preceded, accompanied, and followed by visual ones, so that very soon, by association, the one is equivalent to the other. In fact, as far as scale comprehension goes, the visual contacts go further than the tactile ones, for the visitor can perform only one tactile operation or two at a time, but he can *see* a great many scale indicators almost simultaneously.

Entourage, also, is vital. Just as a train crossing the prairie looks like a toy, so a house set upon a razed site looks like a model, which one hopes will soon be picked up and put away. Shrubbery, walks, and trees (these are even more traditional than the Georgian style, if I may be forgiven for using the word) serve an exceedingly important function in relating the building to its setting and the observer to the whole composition.

Gradually, as the contemporary eye becomes accustomed to new forms and new uses of material, these in turn will become adequate scale indicators. We may, for example, begin to associate certain kinds of fenestration with certain building types. Then glass *areas* (not subdivisions) will be recognized as having such-and-such size. It is necessary for the designer to achieve an awareness of just how much his public is already trained to interpret at a given time, unless he is more concerned with the approbation of posterity! It would seem to me, however, that an effort to divine the visual habits of a future generation involves even more guesswork and fewer opportunities for checking than the sufficiently difficult job of working for contemporary eyes.

In all our discussion of scale up to now I have spoken as though the sizes which the eye expects should be the ones used, or in other words, expectation should correspond with actuality. While it is true that in this way the greatest possible sense of "security" is achieved, there are occasions when a designer sets out deliberately to depart from truth, to fool the eye of the observer by giving it an actuality that is other than what it expects.

Lest this falsification be followed up the abstraction

ladder to the term "dishonesty," I hasten to say that there are sound and valid reasons for this sort of deception.

There are four kinds of scale (size interpretations) used in architecture. The first is the one already considered, "true" or "natural" scale, in which sizes turn out to be those which one anticipated.

A second type of scale is that which is sometimes called "intimate." It is often used for residential work to convey an impression of cozy shelter. Sizes are slightly (but perceptibly) smaller than one expects them to be. This tends to give the observer a pleasant sense of ease; he feels that his environment is readily manageable and that he can relax. Part of his reaction, also, is a gratifying increase in his awareness of his own importance as an individual. He feels larger and more

powerful in an environment whose elements he can cope with so effortlessly. Of course, the observer himself does not go through any conscious thought process such as this. He merely feels a small glow of satisfaction and says, "Charming, charming! I feel at home already." When overdone (which, unfortunately, it frequently is) the intimate scale becomes cloyingly cute. The little greeting-card house, with the eaves that swoop way down to the ground and the ever so tiny, diamond-paned casements, may appeal to some highly sentimental souls, but the average self-respecting citizen is annoyed at an environment that debases itself to such a degree. I have seen little development houses that postively fawn upon you, with a result not too far from nausea.

But when well done, intimate scale can be very valuable. When entering a large restaurant, for example, particularly an expensive one, you do not like to look out over an acre of identical tables and be led to table number 469 Left Field. You do not enjoy losing your individualism so readily—not at $4.50 a head. You want to feel special and be taken to a special table. If the head waiter should greet you by name, so much the better. You may even give him a special tip.

The wise architect makes good use of intimate scale in solving this kind of problem. He cuts his room up, visually, by columns, mirrors, draperies, wall treatment, lighting or a dozen other devices, to create relatively small areas in which tables may be *grouped* instead of ranged. Each table in a group is a "corner table," or a "side table," or a "center table." Whatever its position, it is a "special" table, which, although you know better, you somehow feel has been created "especially" for you.

46

I am putting so much stress upon the word "special" in this connection in order to emphasize the fact that the use of intimate scale is inseparably bound up with the glorification, or at any rate gratification, of the individual. Putting it baldly, intimate scale shrinks the physical setting in order to swell the ego.

Our restaurant illustration can be carried further in developing this point from the negative side. When you are *not* paying $4.50 up, when you are *not* interested in pampering your ego, in short, when you just want a fast sandwich and a cup of coffee (total, 45¢), you pop into a cafeteria, line up at the counter quite anonymously, eat at any table that has a vacant seat, and get out. The "special" table in this context has no appeal to you; it would seem just as much out of place as a counterman in white tie and tails.

Intimate scale can be used to good advantage in theatres, particularly legitimate theatres. When you have bought tickets well in advance and your best girl is looking especially pretty, it is rather a shock to be shown to your seats and feel that you should have brought your telescope. Actually, vision and hearing may be completely adequate, but you should not *feel* far away from the stage. Many architects have handled this problem successfully. A case in point was the Center Theatre at Rockefeller Center, where the use of elliptical horizontal lines tying the balcony to the proscenium made the distance from the back of the house to the stage seem much shorter than it was, shorter, in fact, than many an actually smaller house. Falsification? Decidedly. Dishonesty? Not to my manner of thinking. To me it would be much more dishonest to express the distance "truthfully" and thereby cheat the theatregoer of an evening's pleasure by making him feel that he would have done better to stay home and hear the performance over short wave.

The converse of intimate scale is heroic or monumental scale, in which everything is somewhat larger

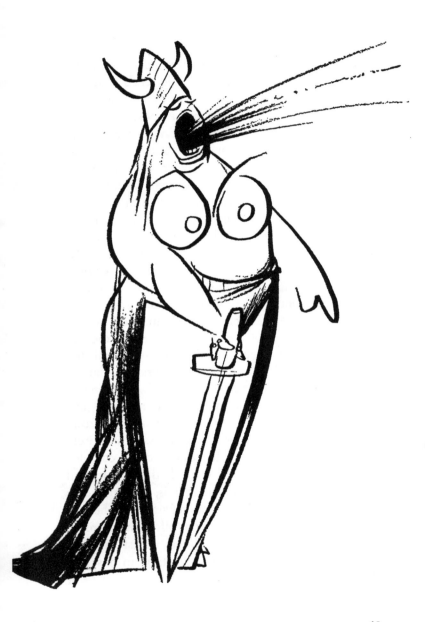

49

than the eye normally expects. It has to be handled with a delicate touch, for if intimate scale swells the ego of the observer, monumental scale tends to shrink it. The designer wants his observer to be impressed, to have a feeling of awe, but not a sensation of oppression or fear, such as he might well have if he senses his own relative smallness and fragility too keenly. The sense of awe must be mixed with pride at being part of, belonging to, or contributing to so important a business. The Lincoln Memorial in Washington is a most successful example of monumental scale which impresses but does not depress; on the contrary, one has an almost soaring feeling of pride. But there are a hundred other buildings in the Capital which you want to get away from as soon as possible.

It is worth noting that both intimate and heroic scale depend utterly upon the existence of *normal* scale in the majority of architectural work. If the eye were not trained to expect certain sizes as normal, the smaller-than-normal of intimate scale and the larger-than-normal of monumental scale would have no meaning at all. In other words, and this is the meat of our scale analysis, a given building has *no inherent scale quality of its own.* Its scale effectiveness lies entirely in the relationship between its scale and the complex of other existing architectural work. If this is true, and I think I have demonstrated that it is, we can never look at an architectural creation separately. There is no piece of architecture apart from all architecture. It follows also that there is no architect unless there be architects. The solitary genius, creating in inspired isolation, does not exist, except perhaps as a state of mind.

50

To the three major scales—normal, intimate, and monumental—should be added a fourth, a minor one which I like to call "shock" scale. It is minor because (perhaps fortunately) its use is limited to very rare applications. Yet when well done and in the proper instance it can be tremendously effective.

We are all aware of the peculiar fascination that people feel for things that are extremely "out of scale." Why do we exclaim over the tiny locomotive, the miniature elephant, the cute little Eiffel Tower that hang from a charm bracelet? Why, at Macy's Thanksgiving Day parade, are we delighted by a fifty-foot

51

Mickey Mouse? Why do side shows feature midgets and giants?

The answer lies in the last question. Side shows also feature bearded ladies and five-legged calves. We like freaks. We enjoy being startled by departures from normalcy, provided we do not take these departures seriously. If we thought for one instant that we really looked the way we do in one of those "fun mirrors" we would not find it very entertaining. And if we thought the fifty-foot mouse coming down Broadway were real, the cries we would utter would not be cries of pleasure.

Shock scale, then, can be used when you want to startle and excite your observer in fun. You will not use it when you want his mood to be serious, as in a library or a cathedral, let us say. You will save your shocks for their entertainment value and use them where entertainment is your purpose—a night club, an amusement park, an exposition building, a merchandising display.

Some aspects of modern commerce tend to approach show business so that sometimes in the reception room of a steel company's administrative building a photomural of a twenty-foot paper clip goes rather well with the bleached blond furniture and the chromium secretaries. This kind of thing is dangerous, however; visitors from abroad, who do not quite share our grim respect for paper clips, have been known to be amused.

The successful use of scale, whether it be normal, intimate, monumental, or shock scale, requires of the architect great deliberateness, awareness, and infinite care. The relationship between what the eye expects, what it sees, and how it responds is extremely delicate.

52

It must be reasoned out by the architect as well as felt intuitively. I am convinced that good scale is never accidental. It is too involved and difficult a matter to just happen. It is always the result of skilled and concentrated effort. Even those architects who design in that extreme of traditionalism known as "out of the book," doing a minimum of personal thinking, are using the fruit of the earlier deliberation of their source designers.

In putting a period to this section on scale, I feel it worth while to recall the triple aspect of architecture described in chapter one: the *intention* of the architect, the *potential* of the structure, and the *response* of the observer. In this matter of scale we can see the three aspects in clear operation. The architect, using all his trained aptitudes, is trying to establish contact with the sensitivities of his observer, using as his instruments the elements of his structure. Moreover, and again recalling the first chapter, the architect's purpose is to evoke a response—awe, pride, gratification, titillation —which is fundamentally *emotional*. Architecture is emotion, I submitted, and scale is a tool for evoking emotion.

Rhythm

One of the most baffling problems has been the peculiar periodicity or rhythmicity which we find in life. Lately, Lillie and others have shown that this rhythmicity could not be explained by purely physical nor purely chemical means, but that it is satisfactorily explained when treated as a physico-electro-chemical structural occurrence. The famous experiments of Lillie, who used an iron wire immersed in nitric acid . . . reproduced . . . a beautiful periodicity resembling closely some of the activities of protoplasm and the nervous system.
Alfred H. Korzybski, *Science and Sanity*

Rhythm

SCALE IS ONLY ONE OF THE ELEMENTS
that make up architecture's potential for evoking emotion. True, it is a powerful one, but rhythm is even more powerful because it appeals to roots of feeling that go much deeper. Scale responses, as we have seen, are largely conditioned. They depend upon what the eye has learned to expect and has been trained to interpret.

The capacity to respond to rhythm, however, appears to be inborn, at least to a large degree. Even the tiniest of infants reacts to hand clapping and knee dandling, and if you have ever suffered the traumatic experience of visiting a nursery school, you will have noticed that the rhythm "orchestra"—drums, pans, boxes, hammers—is one of the few activities in which these little savages can be made to cooperate.

The emotional effect of rhythm is easily verified. From the jungle tom-tom to Benny Goodman's sextette, from the banjo on the levee to Ravel's "Bolero," from the jig of Ireland to the rhumba of Cuba, it is rhythm which makes otherwise dignified people cavort and contort themselves in manners which their rational faculties alone would never condone. At certain revival meetings, rhythm (flavored by religious fervor) has

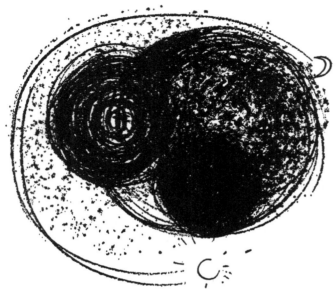

been known to cause frothing at the mouth and rolling on the ground. Many a young man, assuming a glazed and hypnotized look, has marched off to feats of heroism, motivated as much by the beat of martial music as by love of country. What gladdens the heart as quickly as the rhythm of a *paso doble* or saddens it as promptly as the muffled drums of a funeral march?

Rhythm is part of the life process itself. We breathe in rhythm, a rhythm whose tempo accelerates under emotional stress. The same is true of the beating of our hearts. The larger rhythms of sleeping and waking take their place in the yet larger rhythms of the sun, the moon, the tides, and the seasons. Our very existence, the pattern of the generations, is a rhythm, profoundly moving to those who feel it.

Psychologists tell us that in emotional evocativity

the stimulus of rhythm is second only to that of smell, the olfactory sense being the one on which, in pre-human periods, we depended most for self-preservation, for seeking food or a mate, and for distinguishing friend from foe. But aside from a few scattered attempts to squirt perfumes into the air conditioning systems at Radio City, I know of no serious efforts to make use of smell in architecture.

Actually, smell does operate in architecture, even though the designers are unconscious of it. I am sure that the damp odor of masonry in a cathedral, mixed with a faint undertone of candle wax and old prayer books, has much to do with creating the desired mystical mood of the building. In the theatre lobby, does not some of the festive feeling originate in the powder and perfume of the ladies, the aroma of good tobacco, and the fresh ink of the programs?* And as for libraries, who shall say how much scholarly devotion has been inspired by the musty exhalations of old bindings?

These questions may some day be explored, and a new dimension added to architecture. Meanwhile, after smell, there is rhythm, a tremendous tool for achieving not only emotional response but the particular *kind*

---

* Al Hirschfeld in *Show Business Is No Business*, p. 79, describes an opening night: "The crowded outer lobby of the theatre is permeated with a unique redolence. A potpourri of the perfumery of perfumes blended with rain-soaked mink, sweet-scented bath salts, wet new leather, ambrosial hair oils, garlic, pungent Martinis, damp corsages, boutonnieres, and witch hazel. The social importance of the event coincides with the quality of the aroma. The potency of the scent (similar to incense and candles in other temples of worship) has a decidedly intoxicating effect on your senses. You are elated. You are excited. You feel younger, as if you have just washed your feet."

59

of emotional response the architect wants in a given building. For one of the conditioned abilities of the human mind is that of translating a pattern that is perceived *visually* into a rhythm that is felt as though it were being *heard*. The elements or accents of the visual pattern, separated by secondary elements or spaces, take on the nature of beats separated by gaps of time.

Actually, there is a time factor involved in the visual perception of a pattern. First there is the distance between the elements of the pattern, closely spaced elements being scanned more rapidly than widely spaced ones; secondly there is the matter of interest. The eye passes over forms of minor interest quickly, but is arrested or slowed by those which engage its attention. Thus the time gaps which establish the tempo of a visual rhythm in architecture are determined in actual execution by distances, measured in feet and inches, and interest, estimated by examination of the workings of the human mind. The point to be remembered is that the time aspects of visual pattern, however achieved, are identical with those of audible rhythm, so that comparisons of emotional reactions caused by rhythms *seen* and rhythms *heard* are entirely valid.

The most immediate reaction to rhythm is to fall in with it. You "get in step." You tap your foot, you snap your fingers, you join the rhythm. You become part of it in a process which is not so much imitative as absorptive. The mood of the rhythm then becomes your mood. Or rather, your mood becomes that of the rhythm, even when the level of response is beyond that of tapping.

The architect is thus faced with the task of selecting

60

a rhythmic pattern which is expressive of the mood or emotion he wishes to evoke. A very slow and even beat, for example, will put the observer into a frame of feeling suggestive of dignity, majesty, poised assurance—the essense of the sense of monumentality. Consider the Parthenon from this point of view. Note the simple, strongly accented spacing of the columns, the continuous and constant depth of shadow under the cornice, the regular alternation of post and lintel, light and dark. Looking at it, you have the sensation of taking part in some august procession that with measured tread approaches or leaves the building. Not that you actually visualize yourself leading the elders, but without going through any such specific imagery, you perceive the quality of the mood, intuitively and at once.

If the architect wants an effect that is less stately, he will break the even beat by inserting a minor rhythm. Within the solemn dum, dum, dum, dum of his major pattern he will place secondary elements (perhaps windows, statues, or panels) so that the beat becomes dum da, dum da, dum da, dum da. Immediately, although one is still marching, the tempo has quickened; this procession has a gayer quality.

With each added complexity and variation of rhythm, the spirits lighten until a really festive mood is indicated. A World's Fair building, for instance, might well have a rhythm that goes dum, da da dum, da da dum, tra-la-la ta ta, *ping!* The *ping!* of course, is a tower with a flag pole.

When rhythms are unaccented, subtle, and varying, the mood of the observer is no longer being directed in rigid channels; instead, it is being played with, as a

61

story teller, in words or music, plays with the interest of his audience, intriguing it there, soothing it here, surprising it, amusing it, doing everything, in fact, but letting it flag. Such architecture tends to be informal, often even picturesque. Over-all patterns of intricate detail suggest full orchestration, many instruments blending their tonalities into a single rich harmony. Some Byzantine works, with their elaborate surface treatments and mosaics, give this kind of effect.

One of our better known abstract painters tells me that he likes to use sharply broken rhythms, with painfully sudden changes, because he feels that he can in this way evoke emotional responses that are expressive of the unhappy tensions he finds in contemporary life. Society, to him, is highly neurotic, confused, and complex; he chooses rhythms with similar characteristics.

Architects and painters are not alone in suiting their rhythms to the temper of the period. In some of the

62

more advanced modern music, the same jangled sense of crisis can be perceived. Not long ago I was present at the playing of a new composition of this kind. At the end, one red-necked gentleman, who had somehow wandered into the recital, lit a fat cigar and, pointing it toward the musicians, remarked, "They talk about the atom bomb, but you just listen to that and you can *tell* something's going to happen!"

Such rhythmic expressions, of course, come from those individuals who are spiritually uncomfortable, to put it gently, in modern society. In the more "adjusted" strata are found people who are proud of our scientific, mechanized culture and who have faith in the ultimate solution of our problems by means of one of the existing formulae—Marxism, Fascism, or Democratic Capitalism. You will find their assurance demonstrated in the steady rhythms of the buildings they design—the great serial bands of alternating floor slab and strip window, the confident repetition of endless mechanically identical units. In Brazil's Press Building or New York's U. N. Secretariat, there are no nervous fears about the way the world is going. On the contrary, perhaps the clearest thing they express is a fundamental belief in and admiration for organization, statistical knowledge, and the rationale of building techniques. When you look at these buildings and perceive their rhythms, you are powerfully reassured. They are like giant card punching machines into which all the troubles of mankind can be fed, to come out not only solved but neatly packed. And labelled.

Rhythm is essentially repetition. But it need not be repetition of equal elements, however self-contradictory that may sound. It may be the repetition of elements whose *differences* progress uniformly. Thus the units of a rhythmic pattern may get larger or smaller as they go along, varying either by the same amount or in the same ratio. The tempo of the beat is slowing down or speeding up, as the case may be.

We accept augmenting and diminishing rhythms because augmentation and diminution exist all about us as part of the life process, which is one of growth and decay. Every action, every movement, every thought, even life itself, has a beginning, a rise, a climax, a dwindling, and an end. All or part of this sequence can be used as a rhythm, or the whole may be utilized as a *unit* which is repeated.

In many skyscrapers the vertical distances from set-back to set-back diminish regularly, reading from bottom to top. This is a rhythm whose tempo increases as the beats become smaller and more closely spaced. Many such rhythms occur in nature; the first example that comes to my mind is that of a flat stone sent skipping across the surface of a pond. Each successive hop is smaller and quicker, until finally the pattern comes to an end.

The spiral and the volute are similar instances of swelling or shrinking rhythms, whereas the fret or wave shows a complete cycle of diminution being used as a unit in a pattern of equals.

A diminishing rhythm is also a growing rhythm if read in reverse. Objectively, the two are identical, the only difference being at which end of the progression the eye of the observer chooses to start. This is not a free choice, however, as the architect, knowing that the emotional effect of a rhythm read as diminishing is

64

extremely different from one read as augmenting, is careful to force the eye to read in the desired order.

I have been speaking of rhythmic patterns as though they were made up of surface or façade elements, more or less linear in character. This, of course, is misleading, since rhythms are perceived in every aspect of architecture—in the pattern of volumes, the succession of areas of varying light levels, the juxtaposition and weighing of colors and textures. The flow of stresses, sensed if not analyzed in the structure, makes a pattern too. Seen, as a building is, from a multitude of angles —from within and without, from near and from far, by day and by night, under sun and under snow—a piece of architecture offers rhythmic patterns and resulting emotional responses which for richness, variety, and complexity make most symphonies seem almost static.

Of course, the crux of the whole matter lies in the ability of the architect to choose the kind of rhythm that will express the emotion he wishes his building to convey and his capacity to feel that emotion himself in the first place. If the architect designs without the inner excitement that accompanies the truly creative act, if he is unmoved by the import of what he is doing, he will at best select his rhythms by rote; the result will inevitably be as unconvincing as the mechanical sexuality of a bored burlesque queen with a corned beef sandwich on her mind.

That is why the architect who disclaims any special interest in a particular building on the grounds that he is "just doing a job" so often fails utterly to do the job.

On the other hand, the architect who is sincerely stirred by what he is about is on the track of finding, among other things, the rhythmic pattern that will express the emotion he feels. Obviously it will do him a great deal of good to know something about music and the dance, these being the art forms in which rhythm is most closely tied to expression. Conversely, if he is unmusical and thinks dancing is merely silly, perhaps he will be wise to specialize in specification writing and leave design to others, for the application of rhythm to architecture proves, for the thousandth time, that Art is one, and what are called the arts are merely different media.

Originality

> . . . There is, it seems to us,
> At best, only a limited value
> In the knowledge derived from experience.
> The knowledge imposes a pattern, and falsified,
> For the pattern is new in every moment
> And every moment is a new and shocking
> Valuation of all we have been. . . .
>
> T. S. Eliot, *East Coker*

Originality

I HAVE MANY TIMES HEARD ARCHI-
tects say, as they began some new commission, "This
time I'm going to do something really original." I've
said it myself and so have you if you happen to be an
architect or, as a matter of fact, if you are engaged in
any sort of creative work.

But I have never, in my experience, seen any true
originality emerge from an effort that began this way;
sometimes the resulting design is "novel" or "different"
or even "odd," but most often it is no more than a
rearrangement of the latest clichés.

Still, the search for originality goes on; we admire
it, we desire it, we value it above almost all other qualities. With so much time, energy, and attention being
expended on the effort to achieve it, therefore, perhaps
we should find out what it is. It is a good idea, as the
phrase goes, to know what you're fighting for.

The word "origin," of course, means source, or birth.
Originality, then, would refer to that which has its
source in the creator. The key word here is "in." Originality is *in* the designer; it never comes from outside
him.

This much would seem to be obvious; yet the architect who sets out to be original, deliberately, does not

look to himself as a source. Rather, he examines the work of others in order that he may do something different. Thus, if only in a negative sense, his output is determined by sources outside himself, very much as the moves of a losing chess player are determined by the actions of his opponent. He is a follower. Others are telling him what he may *not* do, hence sharply limiting what he *may* do. At the moment of deciding to be original, the architect is already severely handicapped.

So far we have found out where originality has its source—in the designer himself. We have also found out where it does not have its source as far as his own creativity is concerned. But, though we know where it is and where it is not, we still do not know *what* it is.

Let us begin by deciding what it is not. I think we can agree that it is not being "different" or "novel" or "odd." In fact, we use these three words with a distinct connotation of contempt, however mild; but we certainly mean to convey only the highest respect when we use the word "original."

Not long ago a new magazine appeared on the stands, after a considerable publicity build-up. It was called *Flair,* and no one could deny that it was different, novel, and odd. Amoeba-shaped holes were cut in its cover, and it had insets which unfolded in all directions. Some even fell out. The new publication aroused a good deal of interest. People talked about it, and even though some of them made caustic jokes about it, they did not fail to examine each new issue promptly upon its appearance. After only a few months, however, *Flair* folded and died. Why?

I submit that *Flair* failed despite the skill and ingenuity of its editors because it had no point of view, no convictions, other than a belief in the value of an elegant vocabulary of publishing devices. But no vocabulary, however charming, has any more value than the value of the meaning it conveys. *Flair* had nothing to say.

People sense such a lack in architecture just as well as in a magazine. You may design pretzel shaped walls, if you like, and suspend them from a butterfly roof by glass tubes, but if there is no serious substance to what you wish to say by these forms, the best you can hope for is that people will murmur, "Amusing!" as they turn away.

But to make a substantial statement with conviction and authority does not necessarily imply originality either. One may believe profoundly that two plus two equals four and proclaim so in accents ringing with the tone of truth without evoking very many gasps of admiration for one's originality.

Conviction and meaning, then, do not constitute originality. Neither does being "different." We are still left with our first question. What is originality?

The answer, it seems to me, is that while neither novelty nor difference nor conviction alone makes originality, a combination of these qualities does. If an architect finds *within himself* an idea for a novel or different expression *in which he believes profoundly* the result cannot help but be original.

When I say "within himself," I am speaking not only of the necessary source of originality but of the ultimate uniqueness of the individual personality which we have already discussed in connection with the question of style. This uniqueness is of course heavily coated by many layers of commonly held ideas,

71

values, and behavior patterns, the product of a commonly experienced culture. To get through these layers, to give expression to the unique core, is a process requiring much self-development, soul-searching, and stubbornness. It is no small task, especially in a period such as ours, when the pressures to conform are, shall we say, rather substantial.

If the individual succeeds in tapping his unique essence, however, the result must, by definition, be different. But it will not be a "differentness" negatively dictated by others; it will be the complete "differentness" of true creativity.

I have heard many artists, in various creative fields, speak of the sense of being purged, the glorious exhaustion they feel when they have, as they sometimes put it, "given of themselves." It is a sensation in no way comparable to the ordinary fatigue that follows routine work. It is a glow, a rich awareness of fulfillment that is a fitting sequel to the thrill of the creative experience itself, a thrill which we call "inspiration."

This whole business of searching out and releasing the inner soul, the excitement of the process and the glowing relief of the purge, begins to smack somewhat of psychoanalysis and a rather unhealthy preoccupation with the ego. It is not so.

Of course one must admit that in the face of the infinite universe the human creative impulse is sheer, arrogant egotism. But it is a healthy egotism, part of that eternal group of natural impulses which among other things is responsible for the reproduction of the species. The artist who finds such natural ego expression in his work never needs psychoanalysis. On the other hand, those artists who for one reason or another have perverted their creativity in directions which they secretly do not honor often spend a large portion of the fruits of their unhappy toil in trying to find release on the analyst's couch.

The architect, perhaps more than any other artist, sits in judgment upon himself. He exercises his rational faculties in merciless criticism of his inspirations. He subjects every idea to the logic of planning, the exigencies of circulation, the technique of construction, and the dictates of economics. If his inspirations fail to meet the test, he discards them. (I seem to be speaking of the ideal architect.) But if they do not fail, if they stand up under his own harshest scrutiny, he will adopt, defend, and build them with utter conviction.

Here, then, are the elements of originality. The "differentness" which is the inevitable expression of the unique individual who has succeeded in plumbing his uniqueness plus the total conviction that is the result of merciless self-criticism.

These qualities are quickly recognized by the observer, not necessarily by means of analysis, but more immediately, by his own responses. Creativity, as I have already pointed out, is the essence of the life process itself. When faced with a product of true creativity, whether it be a building, a painting, a statue, or a symphony (or a baby, for that matter), one senses the power of the process. Even though vicariously, one feels some of the thrill of inspiration and the glow of fulfillment that were the experience of the artist. That is why originality is so unmistakable and so highly prized. It is faith and fulfillment; it is belief and birth. When we see it, we too believe, and in some small measure, we are born again.

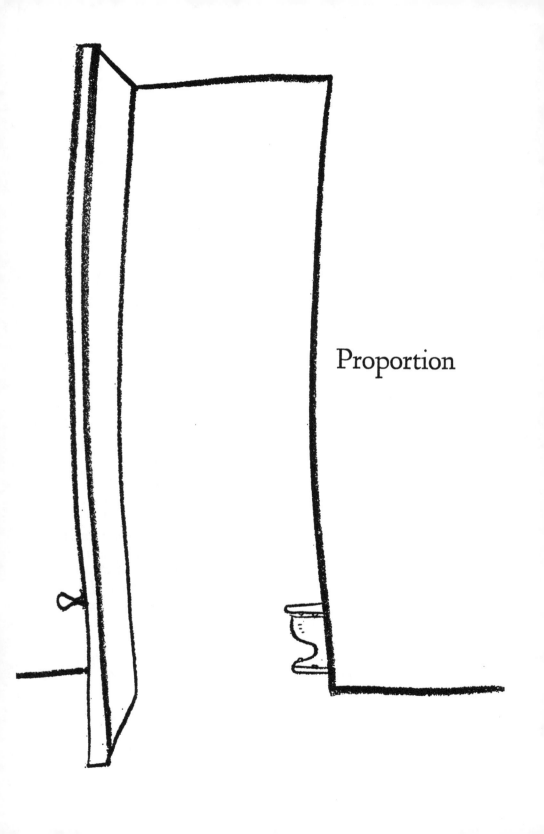

Proportion

It is terrible to see how a single unclear idea, a single formula without meaning, lurking in a young man's head, will sometimes act like an obstruction of inert matter in an artery, hindering the nutrition of the brain, and condemning its victim to pine away in the fullness of his intellectual vigor and in the midst of intellectual plenty.

Charles S. Peirce, *Chance, Love and Logic*

Proportion

ALL THROUGH THESE DISCUSSIONS I
am using the general semantic discipline of attempting
to trace abstractions down to their specific referents,
though I do not often go so far as to employ the
"abstraction ladder." This, however, is a case when the
ladder is perhaps the quickest and easiest way to clarify
the question. Let us set the abstraction "proportion" at
the top of the ladder.

> Proportion
> Width-height ratio
> 30 inches to 6 feet 6 inches
> The bathroom door

Or, we can build the ladder this way:

> Proportion
> Width-height ratio
> 14 feet by 20 feet
> This room

Mr. A., a gentleman we have already met, has his own
ladder:

> Proportion
> Bust-waist-hips ratio
> 34 inches by 25 inches by 35 inches
> Ethel

77

The point is very simple. Just as there is no such actual thing as a muscular giant named Transportation nor a noble lady called Architecture, there is no mystical quality called Proportion. There are only *specific things*, having certain real dimensions—a bathroom door, a room, Ethel. You may profitably discuss the proportions of a door, a room, or a lady, but you cannot talk about proportion-in-general. There is no such thing.

This seemingly elementary fact, however, has escaped theoreticians for generations, with the result that inconceivable quantities of energy and paper have been consumed in fruitless though no doubt fascinating efforts to formulate rules for proportion-in-general; moreover, thousands of architects have botched countless buildings by attempting to follow the "golden rectangles" and "magic diagonals" that were the products of these efforts. Such are the dire consequences of neglecting to find referents for one's abstractions.

It would appear to be fairly obvious that a golden rectangle* which results in a handsomely proportioned

* The word "rectangle" may be considered, to use the language of mathematics, as a variable to which an infinite number of specific values can be given. Thus, as in the expression $2x = 14$, the statement will be true if the value 7 is ascribed to x; otherwise, if some other value is used, the statement is false. *If no specific value* is ascribed to x, the statement $2x = 14$ is neither true nor false; it is meaningless. Similarly, a statement such as "A good rectangle has a length twice that of its width" (or any other such statement) is neither true nor false but meaningless until a specific value—bathroom door, garage door, this room—has been ascribed to the word "rectangle." Only then may it be judged as a true or false statement. In recognizing this apparently simple point, mathematicians are far ahead of most architects, for no sane mathematician would waste a minute arguing the truth or falseness of a purely propositional function.

door can have very little, if any, application to Ethel or to anything else, for that matter, except another and similar door. Each case, in short, calls for its *own proportions*. There can be no formula, however esoteric, that applies to everything. Yet the human mind is often too lazy to think each problem out separately; it prefers to use a formula and, paradoxically, will do an enormous amount of work devising such a formula and then twice as much work defending it.

This is not to deny the fact that there is such a thing as good proportion and bad proportion *for each case*. To make this abundantly clear, just compare Ethel-as-she-is with Ethel-plus-thirty-pounds; or the bathroom door with one of the same height but twice its width.

It becomes necessary, therefore, to consider proportion not merely as a matter of relative dimensions but as a composite result of function, construction materials, scale, and in certain cases, time.

First, function. Since we have been using a door as one of our examples, let us continue with it. The function of a door is to swing open, when required, to allow a human being to pass through a wall having a gap which at other times the door covers. The proportions of the door, the relationship of its height to its width, obviously cannot be thought of in terms of abstract rectangles; both the width and the height are conditioned by the size of the object, in this case a person, that is to be passed through. A garage door, since it is meant to admit cars, must be quite differently shaped. *What is a good rectangle for a bathroom door is not a good rectangle for a garage door.*

Once the rather apparent point has been accepted, it

79

proves completely the futility of the centuries of pre-occupation with golden rectangles and all such mystical nonsense. Not that all problems of proportion can be solved on so simple a functional basis. There are problems of proportion dealing with relationships of volume to volume, of fenestration to wall surface, of light to dark, of texture, decoration, and plain areas; some of these are most complex and difficult. But not one of

them can be solved by general formulae, no matter how many pictures of classic monuments are shown with the cabalistic subdivisions and crisscrosses that "prove" their proportional "systems."

Function conditions proportion, as we have seen. So does construction. Certainly a concrete column which supports a very heavy load will have a different height-width relationship than a post of wood, carrying a light load. The spans will be different, as will the column spacings, the shape of the bays. How, then, could there be such a thing as good column-proportion-in-general? Good proportion, for a specific column, will be to a great extent determined by the nature of the material and the rationale of the structure.

Third, there is scale. As pointed out in the chapter on scale, there is a close connection between scale and character expression. Thus, a room whose proportions are pleasing at, say, intimate scale, would be disastrous if the same proportions were duplicated at monumental scale. To feel the impact of the potential horror in this thought, just imagine your neighborhood Cozie Tea Shoppe, with its low ceiling and narrow doorways, blown up to the dimensions of Grand Central Station.

It is partially by means of proportion that one identifies objects. You recognize a brick, for example, not only by the material of which it consists but by its shape, which means its proportions, length to width to height. You *know* the size of a brick, so you immediately sense the scale of the brick wall or building at which you are looking. Therefore an outsize or undersize brick *in the same proportions* would be a violation of scale, misleading to the eye and damaging to character expression.

Such dimensional relations as those *between* elements—for example, between a door and a window or between one window and another or between a group of elements and another group—could be understood as being involved in the formulation "proportion"; I would not quarrel with anyone who chooses to do so. My own preference is to consider the matter of size and shape relationships between elements rather under the heading of "harmony," "dominance," or "subordination," which I have listed as devices useful in accentuating "unity."

The fourth factor, time, enters when one deals with higher level proportions, the size of one volume in relation to another, for instance. A certain amount of time is involved in the perception and appreciation of a new environment. Let us say that you are designing an auditorium and its lobby. What shall the size relationship between them be? Of course the sizes are initially conditioned by purely mechanical considerations such as seating and traffic capacity (to say nothing of the budget!), but if you are concerned with the esthetics of proportion, you will go beyond these matters. You will realize that the time spent in passing through the lobby serves to *erase* from the mind's eye of the observer the picture of the street outside and his view of the façade of your building. It also *prepares* his eye for his impression of the auditorium. What kind of impression do you want to convey? Continuity? Contrast? You make your decision and adjust the proportions, lobby to auditorium, accordingly. You also adjust other factors, such as color, light levels, circulation patterns, and other considerations of sequence.

Another aspect of the time factor is that of changing

82

tastes with changing time. Ethel's proportions were considered too chunky in the 1920's but just right in the 1940's. At this writing it is impossible to say, but she might well be considered too slim for the 1960's. At the turn of the century, to get back to buildings, when multi-story structures became more usual, people found the proportions of a building that was higher than it was wide somewhat painful. It is easy to see in the façades of that period how hard they tried to cut the visual heights of their buildings with strong horizontal moldings at every story or two and the heaviest possible cornice weighting down the whole. But with the passage of time the public eye became accustomed to the new proportions and even began to enjoy them. By mid-century we were beginning to be concerned not so much with width and height as with volumes—closed, open, light, heavy, free, and interlocking. These are the proportions with which we deal today; happily, no "golden" or "magic" volumes have as yet been imposed upon us.

Sequences

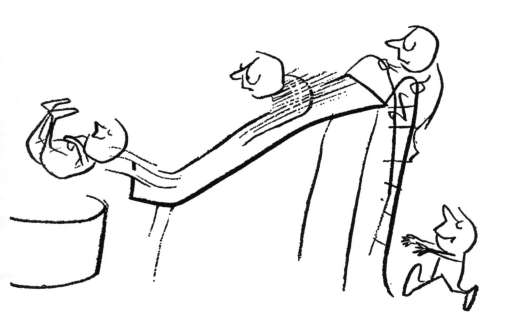

We often think that when we have completed our study of one we know all about two, because 'two' is 'one and one.' We forget that we have still to make a study of 'and.'
A. S. Eddington, *The Nature of the Physical World*

Sequences

I HAVE REFERRED MANY TIMES TO SE-
quences, but have postponed our analysis of them until
now in order first to deal with the factors of rhythm,
scale and proportion, which make them up.

Time and motion are inseparable from the perception
of architecture, which is the basis for my strong disagreement with Goethe's euphonious "frozen music"
expression. You first see a building as you approach it,
from a greater or lesser distance. It may be that your eye
perceives its silhouette before anything else. Or its mass.
Then, as you move closer, you become aware of its most
important elements, its dominant part, perhaps, and its
secondary ones. This moving closer took *time*, time during which your initial impressions of mass or silhouette
became part of your background knowledge, experience
—mood, if you like—thus preparing you for the closer
view.

Such preparation is the essence of sequential art. A
dance which rises in tempo excites you because a previous tempo has been established *from which the rise
occurs.* An orator increases the volume of his voice to
make a point, and the emphasis is successful because a
previous level of volume had been used, preparing your
ear to recognize the impact of the change. The writer

87

uses *italics* with effect because ordinary type face has met your eye beforehand. If he used italics from the beginning, he would have to use roman type for emphasis. In short, that which comes first determines the impact of that which comes next. The second experience shapes the third. And so on.

The abstraction "sequence" when used in connection with architecture has for its referents the actual listing, in order, of the experiences to which an observer is subjected as he moves towards, into, and through a building. And let me repeat, this motion involves time.

Suppose you are the architect for some public building. Your list will go all the way from your observer's first sight of the building to the moment when he transacts the business for which he came, to see a particular official or take a train or look up a reference. Then your reverse list begins, as you take him off his train, away from the official, or loaded with notes. Each item on the list will be examined carefully, the variables considered, the desired effect determined, the time involved estimated.

If the first view of the building is from some distance, for instance, so that details are indistinguishable, the mass and silhouette will have to tell the story, express the basic concept upon which your whole design is founded. You will not be able to depend upon "façade" treatment for that. Also, the building, if seen from such a distance, will undoubtedly be seen by many people who will not go to it at all; not that they are repelled by it; they merely have no business there. For such people the first view is the beginning and the end of the sequence; consequently, it must be a complete experience in itself of a lesser but still satisfying nature. In this

connection you will do well to remember that people who are *not* going to a building have quite a different attitude towards it than people who *are* going to it. Their attention, both emotional and intellectual, is much less involved, and their expectations are met proportionally more easily. Perhaps this is why so many have spoken of the tall buildings of New York as being "impersonal." It is the speaker, having no concern with the buildings, who is impersonal. He feels quite otherwise about the mass of brick and steel he calls home. He may love it for its cool simplicity or hate it for its cold hostility (his domestic life has a good deal to do with this), but it is never "impersonal."

Carrying on with the purposeful visitor, however, there comes a point as he gets nearer the building when he becomes aware of its elements—its colonnade, its marquee, its windows, its entrance. You must establish and to a great extent create this point, for upon its distance will depend the scale treatment and rhythmic delineation. If you estimate this point wrongly, much of your design will not work; it will reach the eye of the observer too soon, while he is still too far away, or too late, when he is already too close. Time and distance in architecture, as in physics, are functions of one another.*

You must also determine, with considerable accuracy, the moment when your observer will want to know

* "The views of space and time which I wish to lay before you have sprung from the soil of experimental physics, and therein lies their strength. They are radical. Henceforth space by itself, and time by itself, are doomed to fade away into mere shadows, and only a kind of union of the two will preserve an independent reality." Hermann Minkowski, *Space and Time*.

where the entrance is. There is nothing so quickly destructive of response to architecture as lack of clarity on this point. If your man feels any doubt at all as to where he is supposed to go in order to get into your building, you have lost the game of sequence, as far as he is concerned, right then and there. His steps hesitate, his brow shows a wrinkle; in short, you have baffled and irritated him. Even though you may have done this in only a very slight degree, you have committed an unforgivable sin, for, leaving out all questions of architectural technique, you have no right to baffle and irritate your fellow man. He has a tough enough time in life without the added burden of your ineptness.

You *must* tell your observer which way to go, even if you have to use printed signs, a last resort to which some of our most distinguished architects have been forced. But you will never find yourself in so desperate a plight. Let me reassure you. All you need do is put yourself in the place of the observer approaching the building. Up to point x your way is clear. From there on you want something to guide you. How far from the building is point x? What do you want to see that will make your path unmistakable? Is point x so far away that the main entrance must be distinguished from the minor and service entrances by columns? A pediment? (Or if these words make you shudder, by piers? A marquee?) By deep recesses? Ornament? Steps? Color? Texture?

If point x is close to the building, perhaps all you will want is a simple bank of street-level doors with handsome hardware. In any case, the expression you select will be based upon your estimate of the distance at which your observer will be ready to see it. Any other

approach to the problem is unrealistic in the extreme and, save for the intervention of sheer chance, doomed to failure.

Very well. You have survived this hazard and brought your man to the entrance. Now he enters. A simple enough matter, it would seem. An instant ago he was outdoors; now he is indoors. That's all there is to it.

Yes, that is all there is to it. But how many architects have failed to realize the tremendous psychological concomitants of that transition! With the passage from outdoors to indoors, the man's whole relation with his environment has changed radically and with it, as was developed in the chapter on scale, his own state of being. A moment ago he was in limitless space, looking at an enclosed volume which he was preparing to penetrate. Of course, he was not feeling it on a conscious level, but he had a sense of free personal choice, mingled with a kind of aggressive purposefulness, which served to *condition his responses* to the building.

Now he is inside it. The space around him is no longer limitless; it is defined by walls, ceiling, floor. Outside is the great world from which he feels, now, sheltered. Or perhaps he feels trapped. In either case, there is no denying that his physical situation, and with it his state of receptivity, has undergone a radical change. If you accept my thesis that the observer's response to architecture is determined by his receptivity, you cannot evade an examination of the state-of-receptivity which you yourself are imposing.

The first effect upon an observer when he enters a building is an abrupt shift in his sense of scale. A volume seems smaller when seen directly after the limitless outdoors than it does when coming from another, pref-

93

erably still smaller, volume. Thus if you are planning an impressive rotunda, assembly hall or waiting room, you had better not let people see it as soon as they enter the building, lest they find it disappointingly puny. What you should do is provide a *transitional* volume, a vestibule or minor lobby, through which your main room may be glimpsed, perhaps, but definitely not felt in its actual size.

Here the element of time appears again. This minor lobby must take long enough to get through to allow your observer to forget the scale of sky and street and to adjust his eye to the scale of your interior. In other words, your transitional volume cannot be *too* small. However, time is not always necessarily a function of speed and distance; we are not clocks, and our perception of time is largely subjective. Ten minutes of a kiss may seem but a flash, but ten minutes of an after-dinner speech an eternity. Or vice versa, depending upon who is doing the kissing and the speaking.

Interest is a function of time appreciation. But it works in a rather peculiar fashion. A small volume, barren of elements to intrigue the eye and with all interest (color, light, texture, decoration, etc.) concentrated beyond, will seem even smaller. For the observer looks ahead to where he sees, or glimpses, things of interest, and ignores the dull space through which he is passing. He may often not even be aware of its existence. But if that space is increased, so that it takes him longer to reach the area of interest, there comes a certain point at which he becomes annoyed—frustrated, the psychologists would say. The dull section then seems larger than it is, very much larger if your customer happens to be an irritable type.

94

In relating your transitional volume to your main volume, therefore, you are not dealing with a simple question of proportion. You are dealing with sequence, with what came first and what came next and how long each event took, which means not merely distance, nor even measured time, but how long each event *seemed* to take, which is a factor of interest. A small space will seem larger if the eye is induced to dwell upon its elements. The enchanting Japanese gardens are good examples of this effect. On the other hand, a large volume can be too interesting, as witness an exposition hall with many exhibits. The eye becomes weary of being attracted so often; there is "too much to see"; the place seems crowded, which is another way of saying that it seems too small for what it holds. Interest, in exactly the same manner as scale impression, depends upon sequence. Just as a volume may seem larger or smaller as a result of the volume that preceded it, so factors designed to intrigue the eye will have more or less interest according to what the eye has just finished seeing.

Here the principle is simple. Interest, like energy, flags and needs to be revived and renewed by constantly increasing doses of stimulant. While these doses, the points of interest in your building, may be alternated for effect with transitional periods of relative dullness, the over-all plan must be one of *rising* interest. Each dose is stronger than the last.

In other words, your sequence will be progressive. And since your building is not without limits, the progression will be finite; there will be a top point, beyond which there will be no higher ones. This top point, this peak of the sequence, is called the climax. Climax occurs in every art form I can think of—music, the dance,

literature, drama, sculpture, and painting. In painting it is usually called the center of interest; but whatever it is called, it is the element to which everything else leads, the main thing, the big moment. If the sequence has been properly planned, it is unmistakable. Even the drowsiest concert audience recognizes the instant when the conductor's back seems to broaden and his baton almost says, "All right, men, this is it!"

Sequence, then, besides being a progression of elements of mounting interest, each of which is a preparation for the next, is in its totality a preparation for the climax. A design will be a total failure if the preparation is inadequate for the climax or if the climax does not measure up to the preparation. To use story-telling parallels, the tale that opens with John Smith, 52, shot in the head, is like the grand fireplace in the entrance foyer, next to the coat closet. Who cares about John Smith? Or the fireplace? Our interest has not been prepared for either, though each could be, given adequate preparation, a satisfactory climax. Similarly, the long, long anecdote which winds up in a small pun is like the great, pillared hall that leads to a breakfast nook. As a friend of mine, an engineer, once said, "You don't use a sledge hammer to drive a tack."

It is a delicate business, this building of a sequence to a climax; it calls for visual imagination and ingenuity to create ever newer, fresher, and more intriguing sights to beguile the eye, restraint enough to hold each effect to its proper degree of impact, stubbornness to let no side issues weaken the central purpose, and boldness and fire to give the climax the final punch it needs.

Architecture is perhaps the most difficult of the arts in which to achieve sequence. In music, for instance,

97

the sequence reads only one way. It is a linear progression which starts at the first note and goes on to the end. It cannot be played backwards. The same goes for literature, drama, and the dance. Even painting has the advantage of being viewed from a static position. Only sculpture shares with architecture the ability to be read in every direction—approaching, leaving, and circumambulating. But, and this is somewhat rare in sculpture, architecture is also entered into, worked in, lived in, and died in.

The complexity of the problem, therefore, requires of the architect, in addition to the qualities already mentioned, a high degree of technical skill in handling matters of scale, rhythm, proportion, light and shade, color, texture, and decoration, in short, those factors which made up what we call "composition," as distinct from "planning" or "construction."

Composition

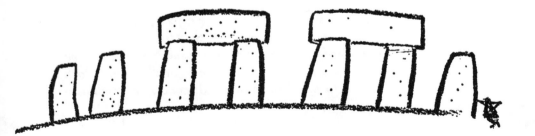

In fact, in structure we find the mystery of rationality, adjustment, etc., and we find that the whole content of knowledge is exclusively structural. If we want to be rational and to understand anything at all, we must look for structure, relations, and, ultimately, multi-dimensional order. . . .

Alfred H. Korzybski, *Science and Sanity*

Composition

THE WORD "COMPOSITION" COMES from roots meaning "together" and "put," so that when you put things together, such as coffee and sugar or bread and butter or even when you shake hands with a friend, you are composing, as far as the literal meaning of the word goes.

The famous monkey with the barrel of type who, given infinite time, eventually sets up all the works of Shakespeare, is composing too. He is putting things together. But the mere fact that a distinction is made between the type arrangement that reads as the works of the Bard and any other arrangement shows that when we use the word "composition," we have more in mind than the literal meaning.

"Composition," architecturally speaking, is a high level abstraction dealing with the putting together of things *in certain ways* rather than in other ways. It is not sufficient to say that it means putting things together "well" or "effectively" or "successfully"; these are abstract terms too and get us no closer to the specific referents which will give substance to our analysis.

When I was a very young man, I studied painting at a famous art school. Our weekly exercise in composition consisted of a study, usually a sketch for a painting

101

of heroic nature. This was submitted for criticism on Monday morning. Sometimes the professor would say the center of interest was too high or too low or that this or that line led away from it instead of toward it. At other times he would merely say "Hm," and let it go at that.

It was all very mysterious, and though we did learn a good deal from it, we never got over feeling like practitioners of some occult trade. Many an afternoon and evening that could have been put to wiser use was spent in arguing the relative dynamics of a straight line and a curved one or in wondering why it is that the most visually important spot in a rectangle is just above the center.

I do not mean to imply that these and similar matters are not worthy ones. On the contrary, a knowledge of optical effects is just as much a part of the architect's or painter's kit of tools as his familiarity with structural techniques in the case of the architect or the behavior of pigments in the case of the painter. But they are no more than devices, means to an end; in themselves they shed no light upon the nature of the total operation: composition.

I have said that though "composition" literally means putting things together, we use the word to mean putting things together not at random but according to a plan, a scheme, a purpose. The purpose of composition is not the erecting of a structure that will not collapse; that is construction. It is not the providing of facilities for a given group of human activities; that is planning. The purpose of composition is to lead the eye of the observer through a pattern of rhythms, effects, and sequences and bring it inevitably to the climax. His eye

102

is not to be allowed to roam at large; its motion, its experiences, are to be *controlled* according to the will of the designer. Just as the composer does not throw all the notes of his symphony into the air and let the listener pick those he wants to listen to and in what order, so the architect does not allow free choice to his public. The musician takes charge of your ears; the architect takes charge of your eyes.

Now, before one takes charge of something, it is wise to find out a little about it, else one might find oneself in the position of trying to lead the bull by the wrong end. It is here that the tools and devices already mentioned have their place.

There is one most important fact about the behavior of the eye, however, that I do not recall coming across in the lectures and writings on composition: the eye can see only that which the owner of it is facing, and not all of that. The actual perception angle is about 160 degrees, a conical segment with the apex at the eye and the axis horizontal, but less than 90 degrees encloses the field of clear vision. In mechanical perspective this is even less, 60 degrees, but the eye, possibly because of its interpretive abilities, can distinguish well up to 90 degrees. This is a rough approximation, of course, since individuals vary a great deal in their visual capacities.

The architect must realize, therefore, that it is useless to design any pictorial effect which involves more than 90 degrees of visual angle, measured from the station point of the observer. It is worse than useless, for any element that is placed outside this 90 degree range will tend to distract the eye and pull it away from the experience planned for it. The 90 degree range is like a frame or, rather, the proscenium arch of a stage, within

which everything the audience is supposed to see must be concentrated. A red exit sign just to the right or left of the stage can wreak havoc with the emotional impact of a tense scene.

What makes the application of this simple rule so difficult is our old friend, time, and that which time involves—space, motion, sequence. Our observer looks at one "picture," then moves to a different position and looks at another "picture." During the moving to the second position, his visual range is shifting more or less freely. At what point can the designer say, "Stop! Now we have our next 'picture' "? The answer lies in the phrase "more or less freely." If the designer has conceived his sequences well and accurately, the observer's eye does not shift freely at all, if by freely we mean at

104

random. On the contrary, it moves *inevitably,* at the *command* of the designer, to the next station point, the next 90 degree range, the next "picture."

Composition, in practice, is not so much the "putting together" of things, as it is the controlled, directed guidance of the observer through a sequence of planned experiences, up to and away from a climax, according to a *definite scheme.*

This much is obvious, but what is not so obvious and what is frequently overlooked is that *the scheme itself must be made apparent to the observer.* I know that in some quarters there will be strong objections to this statement. Does the magician show how his tricks are done? Does the doctor tell his patient everything? Does Macy's tell Gimbel's?

However, architectural design is neither competitive nor curative nor delusionary, to answer these objections in reverse order, though under unhealthy conditions it is sometimes all three. I say that the architectural scheme must be made apparent to the observer because all conveyance of meaning of whatever sort must ultimately be in the revelation of structure, order, and relationships.

A molecule, a bit of "matter," is meaningless until its combination with others in a revealed scheme shows it to be part of a leaf, a table, a fish, or Ethel. The digits, 1, 2, 3, 4, 5, etc., make no sense unless we understand the numerical *order* ascribed to them; 2 follows 1, 4 lies between 3 and 5, and so on. If we were not aware of this order, we could not add, subtract, or in fact do anything with the digits. The structure of numbers, the 10, 100, 1000, etc., relationship is what makes the system a system. To one who does not understand the structure, numbers can never be more than random marks upon paper.

It is the *order* of notes played or sung that makes a melody; it is the *relationship* of notes played together that makes harmony; it is the *structure* of musical elements played in a planned sequence that makes a symphony, a concerto, or an etude. It is the relationship, order, and structure of letters that make words, sentences, paragraphs, and books.

These illustrations could be continued indefinitely or at least until every form of conveyed or perceived meaning had been mentioned. But if we are agreed that architecture consists of meaning both conveyed and perceived, it must necessarily be conceded that it fails if structure, order, and relationship are concealed.

How much of structure needs to be revealed to free it of the charge of being concealed? Must the designer show every beam, every girder, every rivet? Some architects try to do just that. I would say that it is sufficient to show what holds up what. The "how" of it is of little interest to the observer, nor could it be shown in its entirety even if we wanted to. It is enough if the structural *scheme* is made understandable. I recall hearing an elderly farmer say of a new building that he liked the way it was stacked. I asked him what he meant by that, and after some cogitation he explained that he would know how to take it apart if he had to. He would know what came off first, what next, and so on. Whether this was an expression of a concealed wish to demolish the building I cannot say, but I think that in any case the architect had succeeded in making his structural scheme apparent.

Of order and relationship I have already spoken a

106

good deal. At this point I need merely add that order and relationship in a building must be made apparent to the observer not only to convey meaning but also to impress upon him that the building is a planned entity, separate and distinct from all other entities. Although it does not conflict with its setting, it is nevertheless apart from it, as a tree is apart from a field or a ship from the sea. If the order and relationship of molecules which make up what we know as a tree were not *visibly* different from the order and relationship of the field, we would not be able to distinguish the one entity from the other.

To sum up, then, the total purpose of "composition" is to lead the observer through a sequence of planned experiences in the process of which there are revealed to him the structural, ordinal, and relational qualities which make the building an organic entity, distinct from all others, and hence capable of conveying the particular kind of meaning which we call architecture.

At this point it becomes possible to speak further about the "emotion" which I called architecture in Chapter One and the "particular kind of meaning" I have just referred to.

It is my contention that the "emotion" ("meaning") of architecture is a direct and fundamental expression of the life process itself, which may seem at first glance to be a somewhat overstated view but which will become acceptable upon analysis. It must, in fact, become acceptable if we are to understand or explain *at all* the tremendous impact and significance that architecture has had for all peoples, everywhere, all through the ages. Architecture is no gentle amenity, tacked onto a culture; it goes much deeper than that.

107

The first and strongest impulse of all living creatures is to live, to survive, to grow, to reproduce, or, if one likes to think in transcendental terms, to go beyond the "something" to the "all." Without arguing these varieties of formulations, let us agree on a simple negative one: the impulse of life is *not to perish*.

Of course, not to perish is rather a neat trick in this world, one that has not yet, so far as we know, been pulled off. All living things die eventually. But we never cease trying not to die. We never cease looking for ways and means of avoiding this or that hazard, solving this or that problem, discovering this or that secret which will help us to foil extinction for the moment and to continue to live.

In other words, we seek that which spells survival and shun that which denies it, at any rate, the sane and healthy among us do; in fact, to seek survival and shun death is about the only solid standard upon which to judge sanity and health.

Architecture appeals directly to this most fundamental of drives.

What does the cathedral say? It says, "Fear not; your soul is immortal. It will join its Maker for all eternity. You will *survive*."

What does the Capitol say? It says, "Fear not; you are part of a great nation; though you pass on, your country—you, in a sense—will *survive*."

What does the monument say? It says, "The poor body lies here, but the fame and the memory will *survive*."

What does the residence say? It says, "Here is the safe place for the most intimate aspects of personal life. Here love and children (the race) will *survive*."

108

Museums? "Art will *survive*." Libraries? Universities? "Knowledge will *survive*."

One could continue indefinitely with this catalogue and find that in every case where architecture has emotional impact—meaning—this element of assertion that man is greater than his environment, that life is more than a fleeting accident of chemistry and temperature, that, in short, there *is* something of the divine in us, is at the heart of the matter.

The meaning of architecture and the reason why that meaning has emotional power now become clear. One cannot rationalize a sense of divinity in the face of all the observable phenomena around us which point in the contrary direction. A sense of divinity, of being greater than death, is an act of faith, essentially, rather than of reason. Architecture renews this sense, reasserts this faith. That is its meaning, and that is why it moves us.

Functionalism

No satisfactory justification has ever been given for connecting in any way the consequences of mathematical reasoning with the physical world.

E. T. Bell, *Debunking Science*

Functionalism

In its most general sense the term "functionalism" refers to the proposition that man-made objects should take forms suitable to the functions which they are meant to perform. Wheels should be round so that they may roll; floors should be flat to facilitate walking upon them; bookshelves should be deep enough to receive books. In principle there is no argument with this rule, although it is frequently violated in practice!

More specifically, however, "functionalism" has become a label describing the point of view of a particular school of designers whose chief tenet it is that traditional forms should be discarded as obstructive to original thought and that each design problem must be worked out from scratch. To mention bookshelves again: one does not design bookshelves by referring to already existing ones; instead one measures books, the average reach of the human arm, the distance at which titles are easily read, and so forth. On the basis of this information the bookshelves are designed, and if they turn out to look like no other bookshelves on earth, so much the better. That would merely show how "unfunctional" all previous bookshelves have been.

With this approach there is plenty of argument,

much of it heated and more than a little bitter. The opposition, calling itself "conservative" or "traditional," feels that new forms are not necessarily better than old ones merely by virtue of being new. On the contrary, it is convinced that old forms, being tried, tested, refined for many years, and full of associations for the observer, are the ones that have virtue—the virtue of being old.

Actually, this whole argument is an outright case of what is known in semantics as confusion of categories. The term "better" has nothing whatever to do with age, newness or oldness, except in the cases of cheese and wine. In architecture, nothing can be called "better" because it is new or old. Such reasoning makes as little sense as it would to equate "better" with weight or bulk, in which case Boulder Dam would clearly be the "best."

However, the "functionalists" do not claim that their architecture is "better" because its forms are new but because it serves its contemporary needs more accurately. This is a point which deserves examination.

In the years immediately following the first World War, northern Europe, Germany in particular, was in a desperately impoverished condition. It was also badly in need of housing and, in fact, buildings of all kinds. Money for fine materials and skilled craftsmen not being available, architects turned to using concrete in simple, rectangular shapes, concrete being the cheapest material and rectangular shapes requiring the least costly form work. Decorations such as carving, moldings, cornices, and columns were out of the question.

In short, they did what they had to do under the circumstances. But men like to feel that what they do they do for an ideal, a faith, a belief, not out of mere force of necessity, which for some reason is demeaning.

114

They therefore proclaimed their starkly severe designs as the beginning of a revolution in architecture (which it was), as a healthy purge to clear out the debris of the past (it was that, too), and as, at long last, a dedication to the new ideals of man (whatever that means).

The theories of "functionalism" were, of course, not new, but their vigorous espousal by a group of prolific and articulate architects made "functionalism" appear to be a new sun rising above a murky world. Without supernatural insight into the minds and motives of these men it is impossible to speculate over whether they were prophets first and designers second or whether they adopted their crusade to flavor the dry crust of their necessity. We will never know; so although the question may be entertaining, it is completely profitless.

At any rate, here was a new movement, complete with leaders, a discipline, and even a slogan, Form Follows Function. And, as is well known by now, it did not fail to win adherents.

It is in this matter of analyzing function that the factor of human behavior, human choice, enters. Which functions shall we *choose* to study? The easiest ones, of course, are those which are measurable in direct, quantitative terms, such as the number of steps the cook takes in preparing eggs and coffee, the number of shirts that can be stacked on a shelf, how much elbow room a lady needs for dressing, and so on. The same kind of reasoning can be applied to all sorts of buildings. How much desk space does a secretary-receptionist need? How many people will be waiting at any given time for an elevator, to see the boss, to use the washroom?

The early "functionalists" confined their choice of functions largely to those which were capable of analysis in numerical terms. The resulting solutions were undoubtedly efficient, provided that the people using the buildings *behaved according to the pattern set for them.* If they tried to behave in any other fashion, rational or otherwise, the buildings did not work at all. In this respect, by dictating the pattern of behavior that was possible in a building, these "functionalists" might easily have flown a banner bearing their slogan in reverse, Function Follows Form.

Recently I came across a bedroom-bath-dressingroom combination that had been worked out to the last detail. Every step in rising, showering, shaving, and dressing had been provided for with astonishing thoroughness. But if the owner some morning should attempt to dress in some other sequence, the arrangement would

prove so awkward that the poor chap would soon have to go back to bed and start all over again. The whole thing is reminiscent of certain highly involved and calculated traffic intersections, where one wrong turn will force you many miles out of your way.

However, if the "functionalist" tries to provide for all the possible variations of human behavior, he soon finds himself with large areas of undifferentiated space in which it is unlikely that anyone will want to do anything. Besides, his beloved Function-Form analysis rapidly becomes meaningless.

The way out of this dilemma which most "functionalists" have found is to consider not *all* possible variations of human behavior but only the few "reasonable" ones.

This eminently sensible decision, however, has a shocking consequence. In admitting the factor of "reasonable" variation, the door is open for all sorts of intangible considerations, for "reasonableness" cannot be measured nor, in fact, be established at all. And hard on its heels, throwing the whole "functionalist" formulation into a kettle of confusion, comes that other great intangible, "amenity."

Now, "amenity" can mean merely that we like ceilings that are higher than they need to be to clear our heads or that we like a sense of space in excess of our exact mechanical requirements; but it can also mean, since *what we like* has been accepted as a valid factor, that baroque pediments, cornices, and Corinthian capitals are completely "functional," provided they give us pleasure.

Once the "functionalist" has gone beyond the mechanical and measurable to consider the intangibles and

117

immeasurables of human reactions, his whole thesis has collapsed, and his differences with the "traditionalist" become nothing more than a matter of stylistic preference. A Lincoln Memorial patterned after the Parthenon is utterly "functional" if it arouses the desired sense of awe and respect, while a U. N. Secretariat can be called "unfunctional" by the man who gets from it no feeling of the brotherhood of man.

Discussions between "functionalists" and "traditionalists" frequently deteriorate into angry shouting for just this reason. Both sides know, fundamentally, that there is nothing for them to discuss; they can do no more than argue bitterly in a vain effort to impose their likes upon one another.

Yet, if a linguistic revision were possible, a real difference between "functionalists" and "traditionalists" could be established. If it were in my power to do so, I would erase the present definitions of these terms and call a "functionalist" a designer who used any form, new or old, if after analysis he was convinced of its usefulness, measurable or intangible. I would, conversely, call a "traditionalist" any designer who used forms, new or old, *without* analyzing their usefulness but merely because they were being, or had been, done.

Since no one will admit to the latter view and everyone will claim the former, all will be happy, and there will no longer be any arguments on "principle." Instead, there will be discussion, as there should be, over the merits of particular and specific buildings.

Or course, whether they admit it or not, most architects of whatever stylistic persuasion are "traditionalists" according to this proposed definition. The young advanced modern, who uses nothing but the latest clichés,

118

is just as "traditional" as his despised elder whose office files are stocked with Ionic façades by the yard. Thinking is the hardest work in the world, and most people, young or old, avant-garde or old dodo, will go to fantastic lengths to avoid it.

119

Character and Honesty

This above all: to thine own self be true,
And it must follow as the night the day,
Thou canst not then be false to any man.
William Shakespeare, *Hamlet*

Character and Honesty

ALL THE MATTERS WHICH WE HAVE discussed so far—scale, rhythm, sequence, and so forth —are inseparable parts of the total expressive medium we call architecture. To consider them one at a time, as though they had some elementalistic existence, is an arbitrary act; nevertheless, I have chosen to do this for purposes of clarity, hoping that through constant reminder and reference the reader will understand that they are not different subjects but merely various ways of looking at the same one.

It is also an arbitrary act to lump "character" and "honesty" together, as though they were synonyms of one another, which is patently false. There are many occasions when "honesty" is characterlessly dull and when "character" is highly fraudulent.

I have done so because it is my contention that in architecture "character" and "honesty" work so closely together that the one is unattainable without the other.

Through their choices, designers, as well as all other people, reveal their attitudes, opinions, prejudices. I have already mentioned jails and pointed out that merely by looking at a jail one can tell whether the architect thought of penology as the punishment of evil-doers, the storage of society's refuse, or the curing

123

and rehabilitation of the socially ill. Or if he thought not at all and merely copied other jail "types" in the "traditionalist" tradition; that will show, too. Incidentally, "copying" is the word one uses in cases when one disapproves of "research."

Consider, for another example, the typical New England town meeting hall. The approach is low and simple, with at most only a few steps separating the entrance from the street level. The doorway is intimate in scale for a public building and unimposing in detail. There are no gates or fences to keep people out; on the contrary, everything emphasizes ease and naturalness of entry. To come to this building, in the unspoken but clearly expressed opinion of the designer, is an everyday, unremarkable act. Inside, too, the close relationship between the platform and the house states again the right, quietly affirmed, of every individual in the community to take part in—or rather, to *be*—his government.

Contrast this with the palace of a German or Austrian emperor or with Buckingham Palace, for that matter. Notice the grand approaches, the sentry posts, the great gates, the guardian stone lions, in fact, all the flummery, which at monumental scale says, "Keep Out. You are not the government here. You are the governed. Should you be graciously granted the privilege of entering on some special occasion, you had better bend your head and step gently."

Again, as in the case of the New England meeting hall, the attitudes and opinions of the architects require no speech to be clear.

The "character" of these buildings derives from the opinions held by the architects. The opinions, of course,

124

come from the society as a whole, but it is through the architect in the case of architecture that they are expressed. If the architects have no opinions, the buildings will express nothing and will hence have no "character."

What opinions on government do architects hold today? Let us look at the newest governmental buildings and see. They are large, simple, clean in line and surface, mechanically exact in their rhythmic patterns. Do they welcome you in? Do they say, "Keep Out"? Nei-

ther. They do not care about you *as an individual* at all. How you feel about them does not matter one whit. You are a number on a social security form, in an income tax file, on a draft register, in a census report. As your number comes up, so will you be treated, not with love and not with terror but as a number is treated—impersonally.

If any one word can be found to describe the "character" of contemporary governmental architecture, that is it. Impersonal. I submit that whether we like it or not (I certainly do not!) this impersonality is the inescapably clear opinion of the architects.

It is expressed in other ways. No one, for instance, could design a Stuyvesant Town unless he thought of people numerically, as replaceable tenants, rather than as warm, breathing, eternally different individuals.

Of course, impersonality is not the only opinion held by contemporary architects. In Rockefeller Center we see a brilliantly expressed recognition of the glamor of large scale entertainment and big business, and in many private dwellings there is an almost worshipful attitude towards mechanically assured, thermostatically controlled, electrified luxury. Also, quite often, there is a pathetic yearning for contact with a carefully prescribed bit of soil and sunshine.

I would not like to give the impression, which I fear I have, that I am hostile toward the architecture of my period. It is true that I do not like a great deal of it, yet there is much that stirs me deeply, much that is courageous, ingenious, and even inspired. It would be tempting to make a list of the buildings which have so moved me, but that would be both out-of-place and presump-

126

tuous. Therefore, let me mention just one aspect of contemporary architecture to illustrate what I mean. On a recent motor trip I was struck by the rich talent, the flexibility, and the inventiveness of the architects who are designing the new motels. In their efforts to grapple with today's automotive culture they are producing work of fascinating "character." And, to repeat, this "character" is a direct expression of the designer's opinions—what he thinks people feel, want, and like when they go on trips and, as a matter of fact, why they go on trips at all.

Where the architect's opinion is most clear and most clearly formed, the "character" is most definite. For that is what we mean by "character": the clear expression of an attitude or opinion.

It is entirely possible, in architecture as in words, to give the *impression* of stating an opinion, without actually saying anything at all. See almost any syndicated newspaper political columnist. Thus, for example, you may see a metropolitan shop front of rough rubble contrasted with plain glossy areas of plate glass. The statement is simple, bold, full of "character," one is about to say. But one doesn't. Why? The answer is that while the designer is speaking in emphatic terms, he has nothing to tell us. He has no opinion whatsoever about modern merchandising and its role in contemporary society—its fierce competitiveness, its snob appeal, its stress on service, the range and variety of the goods it offers. He takes it for granted. And although his design may be skillful, it is thoughtless; its "effect" is an empty one. The pushcart peddler, arranging his paltry wares to catch the eye of the casual passerby, has a greater

127

awareness of what he is doing. His design, nine times out of ten, has "character."

Opinion or lack of it cannot be concealed or falsified. A true believer in the equal worth of all individuals can no more design a good palace than an irreligious person can design a good church, for the basic assumptions upon which conviction, inspiration, and "character" depend are missing.

This is where "honesty" enters. Just as opinion or the lack of it cannot be concealed, so an insincerely assumed opinion shows its hollowness. Its falseness rings out like the pear-shaped tones of a radio announcer reading a commercial. Although he puts all his persuasiveness into it, we know he does not mean a single word.

Opportunism or expediency work no more successfully in architecture than they do in world affairs. Show me an architect who says, "Well, of course, I don't subscribe to this sort of thing, but it's what the client wants, and after all, a job is a job," and I do not need to look at his work. I know it will be meaningless.

When, on the other hand, the architect "honestly" strives to find solutions that fit the world *as he sees it,* his sincerity will shine through irresistibly, overcoming even lack of skill. To use radio as an illustration again, witness the unmistakable timbre of truth that comes through in an occasional candid interview.

The architect, or anyone else, for that matter, who attempts to cope with contemporary problems as he understands them is trying to establish some sort of rapport between himself and life. This is a healthy, natural, sane process through which all living creatures from the

128

amoeba to man must go in order to survive, reproduce, and create.* Any effort to evade it is a sick effort, a step towards decay and eventual extinction.

Thus sincerity ("honesty") is the essential ingredient of "character." Coupled with technical skill and that facility which we call talent or aptitude, it will result in work that inevitably has "style" and "originality." If what it has to say is of universal consequence, it will be "great" architecture.

* "In the end we must live by the nature of things and not by illusion." George Bernard Shaw, Preface to "Getting Married."

CPSIA information can be obtained
at www.ICGtesting.com
Printed in the USA
BVHW082111180219
540594BV00022B/686/P